WITHDRAWAL

KNOW WHAT MAKES THEM TICK

•••••○•••○••• **KNOW** WHAT

KNOW WHAT MAKES THEM TICK

MAKES THEM TICK...

How to Successfully Negotiate Almost Any Situation

MAX SIEGEL

with G. F. Lichtenberg

An Imprint of HarperCollins*Publishers*

HARPER   www.harpercollins.com

HarperCollins books may be purchased for educational, business, or sales promotional use. For information, please write: Special Markets Department, HarperCollins Publishers, 10 East 53rd Street, New York, NY 10022.

FIRST EDITION

Designed by Joy O'Meara

Library of Congress Cataloging-in-Publication Data

Siegel, Max (Max L.)
    Know what makes them tick : how to successfully negotiate almost any situation / Max Siegel with G.F. Lichtenberg.
        p.   cm.
    ISBN 978-0-06-171712-3
    1. Negotiation. I. Lichtenberg, G.F. II. Title.
    BF637.N4S54   2010
    302.3—dc22
                                                            2009030443

10 11 12 13 14   ov/rrd   10 9 8 7 6 5 4 3 2 1

To my mother, the late Delores Frazier,
and to my father, the late William "Bill" Siegel.
Without your love for each other I would not be here.

CONTENTS

PREFACE

PEOPLE ALWAYS ASK ME how I did it—how I got from where I started to where I am today. And to be honest, when someone asks about my success it can still be hard to believe they're talking about me. Back when I was a teenager in Indianapolis, if you had looked at me from the outside, you would have seen a poor black kid with a Jewish name, a mixed-race boy from a broken home—an outsider even among outsiders. My father, who was white, kidnapped my sister and me from my mother, who was African-American; when he died of cancer and she finally found us again, the life she brought us home to was full of addiction and violence—straight ghetto. With a start like that, plenty of people might have expected me to drop out of high school, deal drugs, and end up who knows where. But that wasn't what I did.

I finished high school, then college, then law school, becoming the first African-American to graduate from Notre Dame School of Law with honors. I founded a law firm specializing in sports and entertainment, in time representing Reggie White, the football legend; Tony Gwynn, the greatest hitter in baseball; as well as John P. Kee, Fred Hammond, and other ministers and stars of gospel music. Our success representing musical talent led to the chance to found a small record label that achieved unprecedented sales. In time I became president of Zomba Gospel/Verity Records, the biggest gospel label in the world, and it became one of the most profitable divisions at Sony/BMG. Industry-wide, Christian music sales doubled to over $700 million a year, with gospel leading the way. *Newsweek* named me "the most important exec in gospel music."

At Sony, I served simultaneously as the senior vice president of the Zomba Label Group and a member of the President's Council—the global management team of Sony BMG Music Entertainment—helping to handle the affairs of a company that does five to six billion dollars in annual global revenue, and overseeing the careers of stars such as R. Kelly, Justin Timberlake, Usher, and Backstreet Boys. I began receiving invitations to speak on success and diversity at megachurches, legal and business organizations, conferences on music and on sports, and youth organizations.

In the midst of all this, I was approached by Dale Earnhardt Inc. (DEI), the best-known name in NASCAR. As a boy, I grew up hearing the sounds of the cars on the Indianapolis Motor Speedway. I had loved racing since I climbed on my first tricycle, but it was always a sport where the faces were mostly white. Teresa Earnhardt, widow of the greatest driver in the history of the sport and owner of its best-known team, asked me to become their first ever African-American hire—as president. Then in 2009, I took over management of NASCAR's Drive for Diversity program, working for the entire NASCAR industry to broaden participation at every level and serving as spokesperson for the world's second-largest sport.

If you're reading this now, it's because you want a deeper understanding of success. Of course, you have your own story. It may not sound anything like mine. You may be just starting out, or perhaps you are already well established; you may have more advantages than I did or even fewer; you may have business on your mind or love, family, or spirit. But what I have learned, and what I want to share in this book, is that there are essential rules of success that hold true for us all. They are the rules I discovered—through trial and error—for getting people of all kinds, no matter what their agendas might be, to work with me and to link their successes to mine. How? By tapping into the deep motivations we all share.

What do I mean by deep motivation? I mean the basic human needs and goals that move all of us to commit. Most of the time, they stay hidden. Most small, everyday decisions get made at the surface. For example, if you and I happen to meet today and you're friendly to me—if you make me laugh, compliment the talk I just gave, or say something nice about my kids—I'll probably chat with you for a while, if I have the time. We may exchange business cards, even say we'll be in touch. Someone watching us from across the room might think we have a relationship, and we do, but its motivations don't go deep. They're all on the surface. Because tomorrow if you call that number on my business card and ask me to give you a job, invest in your business, or fly across the country to help you out of a jam, I may still think you're charming or interesting or funny, but I'm going to tell you no. You haven't moved me to commit to you.

The only way to change my mind is to appeal to what really moves me, deep down—the reasons I get up in the morning when the alarm goes off, the reasons I keep on going when I feel like I'm about to drop. Maybe I'm driven to fulfill a dream or to take better care of my family. Maybe I have a passion to express or a moral need to right a wrong. Maybe I have a spiritual calling. Maybe I just want *someone* to give a —— about me. Which is it? What really makes me tick? That's what you have to know. And when you know it, you need to show me how your success will help me realize those deep goals that motivate me. You need to show me that not as an abstract idea, but as a reality I can feel because it's part of everything we do together. If you can't do that, you're not going to get very far with me.

I've been an outsider for most of my life, but I've learned that people will work with you—whoever you are—if you tap into their deep motivations. They will help you reach your goals, and they'll be glad to do it. Because when you really get at the core of what makes a person tick, what motivates them and makes them feel good about their lives, then you can take care of them. And if you take care of them, they will take care of you. The forces of deep motivation are so strong that anyone who learns my rules can succeed, no matter who you are or where you start out; in fact, as my experience shows, if you're starting out from the "wrong" place, or if you've had some success but you still feel like an outsider, then that might just become your biggest advantage.

How did I go so far after such a rough start? None of my successes came according to plan, at least not any plan I made—and I've written dozens of business plans over the years. I got as far as I did by following the rules I will lay out here, rules I learned from some of the worst experiences in my life. Those hard times taught me what makes me tick, and how to work with people's deep motivations to build a more successful life.

I LEARNED THE FIRST of my rules, *know what makes them tick,* when I was twelve years old, when I saw my father for the last time. He had always been a strong, proud man, a charmer with a thick head of dark hair and a full mustache, but when the orderlies brought him home from the hospital he was bald and weak and nearly wasted away. They had to carry him up the stairs in his wheelchair, but lifting him was no trouble—cancer, chemo, and radiation had worn him down to eighty-eight pounds. They rolled him to the table and I sat by him as he said what he had come back home to say. His cancer treatments had failed. "I don't want you to see me looking any worse than this," he said, "so you're not going to see me again."

I was a kid. I didn't know how to answer him.

Besides his sickness, he was wracked with guilt and full of apologies. He apologized for being gone so long on account of his illness, and for traveling so much as a music salesman back when he was healthy. He apologized for leaving my sister, Traci, and me with my stepmother and all her struggles with drugs and alcohol. Since he went to the hospital, she had been carrying on with one man and then another, leaving no one to look after us. One of my clearest memories of those months was how Traci used to cry because there was no adult in the house to comb her hair. She was still small, but even so she had a sense of style. When her hair got tangled, I combed it out for her.

"You may think I don't know what's been going on around here," my father said, "but I do. And I know I can't leave you and your sister on your own with her anymore. So here's what I'm going to do. Downstairs in the closet you'll find an envelope. Inside there is ten thousand dollars in cash and one hundred blank checks that I've signed. When bills come in, if your stepmother doesn't take care of them, you just write in the amount of the bills on the checks, put the checks in the envelopes, and send them off. You're the man of the house now, and you're going to get through this and take care of your sister. But the minute you get word that I've passed away, stop writing checks, because people will know I'm not writing them anymore."

When the orderlies took him to travel back to the hospital, the task he had set out weighed heavily on me. Another kid might have thrown the cash away on some foolishness, or cracked under the sadness and the pressure, maybe by telling the stepmother about the money, hoping she would handle things like she was supposed to do. But not me. My father knew what made me tick: he knew I wanted to believe in authority; he knew that my sister Traci was as important as anything in my world. So when he set me this task, I completed it. I made sure there was food for Traci and me to eat. The rent got paid every month, the water kept running, and the phone stayed connected. Now and then one of the neighbors looked in on us, and Traci and I got by that way until one day in September when the phone rang. Somehow I knew right away that my father was gone. He was thirty-eight.

At the end of his life, he looked like nothing but a powerless, dying man. Some people might even call him a failure as a father. But because he understood my deepest motivations, he moved me to help him fulfill his last responsibilities even as he lay in his hospital bed, helpless and dying. I did the work of a much older person because he appealed to what, for me, mattered most. It was only later that I realized he had done something more. He had shared with me what he knew about being a survivor and a success, what I now call my first rule: *know what makes them tick.* I've lived by it and succeeded because of it ever since.

I learned the second rule, *see where you want to be, not where you are,* when my mother brought Traci and me home to Indianapolis to try to make up for lost time. Our new home was a two-bedroom ranch house that we shared with my three stepbrothers and my stepfather. My parents worked two or three jobs each, trying to support all of us, so there wasn't much free time anyway, and on top of all that they were alcoholics. My stepfather drank nearly a fifth of Old Grand-Dad almost every night, then got up at four in the morning and went to work. Somehow he always provided, but now my mother was spending all her time with her kids by another man.

One night when I was fourteen, I climbed up to the front door, not even sure I should go in. I stood outside listening, as I always did, for music. Music was my cue. If I heard rowdy blues coming from my mother's record player, then inside I would find a drunken bash—and worse. It was better to turn around and try to stay at a friend's house or even take my chances on the street, until the adults finally fell asleep. But if I heard jazz or if my mother had her gospel music on, then everything was cool. Even if the adults were drinking, they would probably just get quietly drunk and fall asleep. The music told me when it was safe to come home.

That night I stood outside the door and listened, but I heard nothing. Three nights before, after an argument, my stepfather had gone out and never come back. I wondered if I should just leave, but it was cold out. I couldn't stand by the door all night waiting for musical cues. I went inside and found my mother alone in the kitchen with the dog. Then I went into the bedroom, and that's where I was when I heard my stepfather come in after three days of being out who knows where. He was a big man, six feet two, nearly two hundred pounds—a World War II vet and former ballplayer in the Negro Leagues. I could feel his heavy step as he moved through the little house. Through the thin walls I heard him talking to my mother in the kitchen. He asked her to put her dog out for the night.

I was hoping that the argument would have gone away by now, that they would just relax and go to sleep, but my mother said, "That dog's not going anywhere." Then I heard her start to pick at him. She was getting into it about the dog, but it could have been anything. Whoever you were, my mother could read you in five minutes, find out your weakness, and work at you like Chinese water torture. She definitely knew what made my stepfather tick, and she was set on using it against him, pushing him and pushing him about that dog.

A kettle was whistling on the stove but no one was picking it up. I heard my stepfather start to yell. When he really got angry, he used to stutter. "*God-dammit-uh-god-dammit-uh-god-dammit, baby! Luh-leave me alone!*" We weren't like other families, where the parents did a little yelling to blow off steam and then settled down again. In my house, when those two got started, there was no way to know where it would end. My older brothers were out; only Traci and I heard them. I was scared out of my mind.

They both yelled at once. The teakettle was still whistling like crazy. I could hear in his voice that he was going to go after her, and without even thinking I ran to the kitchen, trying to be a man and protect my mom. My stepfather was too big to take on, but sometimes I was the only person, including his own kids, who could break up a fight of his and get things under control. If he was out drunk he wouldn't let anyone drive him home but me. I had a kind of influence with him.

I got between them, trying to talk my stepfather down, but my mother wasn't interested. "Mind your own business!" she told me. Then she went back to yelling at him. And I watched him grab that boiling kettle off the stove and bust her over the head with it.

There was blood and terrible screaming. My mother got to the phone and called the police, saying there was a man in the house who had attacked her, referring to him as if he were a stranger. He went into the bedroom and came out again wearing his bathrobe. Then he just sat down on the couch like nothing had happened.

When the police arrived, my mother yelled for them to get "that man" out of the house. They asked him what he was doing there and he said, "I live here."

"You live here?" one officer asked.

"Yeah," he said. "I live here. This is my wife."

The officers looked at each other. By then, things had quieted down. They explained that they couldn't interfere in a domestic dispute, like they were acting some lines from a television show. And then they were gone.

After they left, my mother went to the hospital. She was banged up pretty bad. When she finally came home, no one said much of anything. We were back to "normal," I realized. This was just how it was going to be. But as the night went on I kept thinking to myself: *No. This can't be my life. This isn't where I was meant to be.*

I swore to myself I would make a family one day that wasn't broke, drunk, and violent. I promised I would make a success of my life: I would take on any responsibility, do whatever it took, and I wouldn't stop until I had money, a safe home, a loving family—and no more craziness. To some people, I know, those dreams might sound too conventional, but to me that was what mattered. It's as true for me today as on that awful night. That's what I'm about. That's what makes me tick.

I wanted that better life so badly I could just about see it in front of me, and seeing it, I believed I could get there. I felt I could move out that night, get a job, and support myself if I had to—my picture of my future self was so strong, it made everything that was wrong in the present seem to lose its power. It didn't matter that I was still a frightened fourteen-year-old in a house full of crazies. I was starting to realize that I had gotten through hard times before, that I could worry less that I might not make it and focus more on what I could learn to make me stronger the next time. That was when I understood the second rule: *see where you want to be, not where you are.*

But how to get where I wanted to be? After what my stepfather had done, I felt I could start by killing him, but I knew that wouldn't do any good. So what would? Nothing in that house was going to change. No matter how much I loved my parents, I couldn't fix them. And even if I went out on my own, what skills did I have? Honestly, what did I even know about success? Maybe my dream was nothing more than an empty wish. It seemed as if I had nothing.

And yet, I had my two rules: *know what makes them tick,* and *see where you want to be, not where you are.* As I began to live by them, I began to feel for the first time that behind the craziness in my life there was order and purpose. Even at fourteen, I could tap into it. How? With what I already had: my desire to make things better, my attention, my commitment—my willingness to learn what moved people so they would help me become my vision of my future self. Though I was not a churchgoing kid, I was making a kind of spiritual discovery. Maybe what I needed most had been provided for me.

Once I began to grasp the power of knowing people's deep motivations, I found that my own childhood—the soap opera that seemed to offer so little—was really a treasure chest. Because when your family is black, white, Christian, Jewish, affluent, middle-class, poor, and spread halfway across the country, you learn that while people have their differences, their deep motivations are the same. And no matter what they aspire to or what motivates them, they need help to reach their goals. If you show them you can help them, they will help you, too. I realized that the rules I had learned within my family would work with everyone I met.

I had lost close family young, and there was a lesson in that too: when people are gone, no matter what they might have done, you feel the loss. That experience showed me early on that you don't throw people away—even if they disappoint you, even if they do you harm. Everyone has value, and everyone can be part of your success once you learn where your deep motivations overlap. So I started with the people I had around me—family, fellow students, neighbors, teachers, and coaches. I set out to learn what made all of them tick and to work with them to get out of where I was and into my future. I realized that if I wanted to succeed, it was my responsibility to find the positive potential in everyone I dealt with, to discover what we could accomplish together no matter how different or how difficult they might seem. That's how I found my third rule: *appreciate everyone.*

Following that rule, I've made it my business to work with as many different sorts of people as possible. I've brought professional ballplayers to Wall Street to talk with stockbrokers about making split-second decisions, a challenge they both share. I've brought hip-hop, R&B, pop, and gospel musicians together, crossing all kinds of lines, to take the music to beautiful and profitable new heights. I left New York City and joined DEI as its president and only executive of color, in an industry—racing—known for being Southern and white; in my first year ESPN named me, the outsider, as NASCAR's "Executive of the Year."

For a while, I commuted to my job from my home in Indianapolis, because I felt it was best to keep my family where our relationships went deep—and best for me to do whatever was best for them. It's still true that deep down, if my family is safe and satisfied, then I'm satisfied. That's the power of deep motivation.

In all these ways, I owe my success to the rules I've learned. And in *Know What Makes Them Tick*, I offer these nine rules to everyone, the three I've just shared and six more:

- Show what's in it for them
- Use your outsider advantage
- Gather your inner circle
- Find your ambassadors
- Remember who you are and where you come from
- Change their minds and uplift the community

I provide examples of each rule in action and specific, practical advice to give you the skills you need to hear what motivates people—and to use that knowledge for mutual benefit. Just as I do when I speak about success, touring the United States, England, and the Caribbean, I try to explain these rules in ways everyone can catch, from singers to ballplayers, from factory workers to lawyers, whether they went to Howard University, Harvard University, Community College, or the School of Hard Knocks.

I feel called to share what I've learned because I've observed that when someone offers to share what makes them tick, most people don't see the opportunity they've been given. They don't listen, or they don't make use of what they hear. Instead, these days, I hear a lot of talk about new approaches to "networking." I see a lot of people staking their futures on little chitchat techniques they use at business gatherings in order to "connect." Those approaches are all right as far as they go, but if all you do is ask people to tell you their latest golf score or their new favorite restaurant, you're giving a dangerous signal that can wreck your chances for success. You're saying that you want to keep things strictly superficial.

Why is that so bad? I think of it this way: networking may get you a first date. Connecting may get you a friendly kiss goodnight. But when you're trying to build your future, a kiss won't cut it. You need to do more than make people feel that you're an appealing person, an exciting connection. Success depends on other people *committing* to you, signing on to try things your way: your job application, your new idea, your plan or project or deal. You need them to tie their success to yours. They'll only do that if they feel that you understand what matters to them, and that your success will make them successful, too.

Now here's the good news. It's simpler than you might think. You don't have to be a doctor of psychology to find out people's deep motivations. The fact is, people *want* to share what moves them—if they can find interested listeners they can trust. It's rare in the work world to find people who listen with real interest and respect, who don't use every minute to show off their own charms, push their own agenda, or make their own sale. So I'll give you simple techniques for putting people at ease on breaks and over meals, to make them know you care about what they do all day and what makes them keep showing up for work. You'll learn to show people that you get them, not by imitating them like a chameleon, but by showing respect for their concerns. I'll demonstrate the value of open-ended questions for drawing out people's deep concerns, and the power of nonverbal communication to make people feel safe to share what moves them. You'll stop listening just to prepare your next remark and start listening to understand what makes people tick.

As you master this approach, I'll guide you to gather an inner circle of friends, colleagues, and mentors—like a surrogate family devoted to your success and bound together by the strength of your shared motivation. Then I'll show you how you can build on those shared motivations to uplift yourself, your organization, and your whole community.

Here's what I won't do. I won't put words in your mouth or pretend that there is a step-by-step recipe when there is not, because what matters most is that you find the natural ways for you to live these rules, so you can work with people's deep motivations out of your own genuine commitment. My rules work when you make them part of who you are, letting them inform every conversation you have and all the work you do. When you embody these nine rules, people will feel that you are different. You are worth their effort and their commitment because you're not just in it for yourself. You want to be part of their success. And if that becomes a truth about who you are, then people will respond to that truth, and you will see the results.

Here's an example that might seem small, but suggests something big. Imagine we're having a conversation and your cell phone rings. You look down and see that it's an important caller. What do you say as you interrupt me? You might say, "Oh, I have to take this," which is factual, or, "Excuse me just a minute," which is polite. But you

might also say, "Let me handle this. Then we can talk without interruptions." That last choice tells me that you still have my interests in
mind. I want your attention and even though you're turning that attention elsewhere for now, you haven't forgotten me.

Now, of course, by itself that response I've just described is only a
line. Anyone could use it. But if it's true to your dealings with me, and
true to the rules in this book, I will *feel* that truth. That can make all
the difference in the world.

I TRAVEL FROM CITY to city and corporation to corporation, talking about my rules for success, and people often ask: don't our jobs
and our lives move too fast these days for us to be worrying about
everybody's deep motivations? We all shift jobs more, move around
the country more, work longer hours, and spend more time facing
the screens of our computers and handheld devices rather than sitting and talking with the people we know. Hasn't technology changed
everything? It seems at times as if everyone is replaceable. Do you really believe it's worth the time to learn what each person cares about
most?

I know that when you meet someone today, you have no idea
where he or she will be three jobs from now. But that person may just
be the one person you're going to need later on. He or she might be
the influential decision maker who's going to help you prosper, the
coach who's going to help you get back up if you stumble—or the
mentor who's going to help you keep your head when you succeed.
And the next time you reach out to that person, whether in a day or
in a decade, you'll need to show that you still know what moves them.
Technology may whisk us around the world and give us new ways to
communicate, but there's nothing new about what motivates our deep
commitments. So in our sped-up world, this approach is more rare
than ever—and even more valuable.

Instead of getting distracted by the technological flash and hyper-
mobility of our lives, I focus on learning what makes people tick. It

took me years to make my principles into a practical program; now I want to share it with you so you don't to have to reinvent the wheel. These are the same principles that have guided me at work and at home, the same approach I took with the Fortune 500 companies I've helped manage and all those whose careers I've helped guide, from world-class athletes to recording stars, prominent religious leaders to top business professionals, leading attorneys, friends, and family both around the world and in my own home community of Indianapolis.

I've always believed that if I'm meant to have success, it's so that I can help others succeed as well. I may be passionate about sports and music and family, but there is nothing I'm more passionate about than helping others succeed. That's another part of what makes me tick. I've written this book to reach you, so you can achieve more of the success and satisfaction meant for you, doing good that I couldn't do alone. And when you do, we'll all be the winners.

KNOW WHAT MAKES THEM TICK

CHAPTER ONE

Know What Makes Them Tick

WHEN I BECAME PRESIDENT of Dale Earnhardt Inc., the best-known team in NASCAR racing, it seemed my first challenge was to beat the other side in a complex contract negotiation. Dale Earnhardt Jr., the son of the most famous driver in the history of the sport, wanted to take control of the company run by his stepmother, Teresa, who was my boss. Dale Junior—everyone calls him Junior—was now the sport's best-known driver and its most significant source of merchandise revenue. He said that if his new contract didn't give him a controlling interest in the company, he would leave.

When I showed up, nine months into difficult negotiations, the binder of legal documents waiting for me to review was twelve inches thick. Every day, I was getting calls from legal and business experts, some of the greatest Ivy League minds in the field, telling me how I could structure the agreement in some innovative way they had devised. I heard about reverse equity deals, this kind of trigger, that kind of incentive—all sorts of highly complex compensation mechanisms to get Junior paid on our terms. Meanwhile, we still had no deal. The situation was only getting worse. My phone rang all day long with reporters looking for personal gossip about the Earnhardt family. This new job was like being thrown into a hornet's nest. And to top things off, before I even met him, I read in the paper that Junior didn't understand what Teresa was thinking when she hired some music company executive to run the company.

Of course, I had been hired to do much more than resolve this one dispute. As president of global operations, it was my job to help us win at the track, build relationships with our sponsors, burnish our public image, and transform DEI into a full-fledged entertainment company to set us apart from our competitors. In the longer term, my goal was to help NASCAR expand beyond its traditional white, Southern fan base, building the bridges that would make it a truly national sport open to everyone. But when I arrived, all those goals were eclipsed by the negative publicity of the contract negotiation. It was the number one story in the sport. Journalists spent more time writing about the fire that burned down Junior's mother's house when he was six years old, and speculating on what it meant to him as a little boy to lose his childhood home and go live with his father and stepmother, than on the races themselves. They were exaggerating the present hostilities and creating an ugly image of a family feud. This was the last thing we needed as we worked to show America how racing had grown.

So how did I prepare for my first meeting with Junior and his sister Kelley (who was his manager and one of the most powerful executives in the sport)? I put all the legal proposals aside. I stopped thinking about my next move in the contract negotiations and focused on learning what made Junior tick. Most of all, I listened. I listened to my new boss, Teresa, and to everyone else in management who could give me perspective on the situation. I read everything I could find about his career, watched all his DVDs, and learned all the background I could about the Earnhardt family in NASCAR. What was I looking for exactly? I didn't know yet. Whatever would get me to his core, to what motivated him and made him feel good about his life. To succeed in this negotiation, I had to know what made him tick.

I was excited to meet the charismatic, powerful young racing star I had learned about, but at our first meeting he didn't exactly turn on the charm. His body language was stiff and suspicious, and his answers to my questions were clipped. He barely met my eyes. And so there we were in Junior's office. I suppose he and Kelley were expecting me to make a proposal, or at least to feel him out about some possible terms of his contract. I didn't do that. Instead, I said, "Look, let's put all the papers away. Before we can even start to talk business, we need to know each other. Let me tell you a little about me."

Junior and Kelley seemed surprised, but I went on and shared a story about my family—the one I shared with you in the preface of this book—about my father taking my sister and me away from our mother, about the difficulties after he died and my struggle to put the past aside and focus on building a successful future. I was trying to show Junior that I could appreciate him not just as a business opportunity but as a person I could relate to. If I could show him that I "got" him, then I could show him that I understood what he needed—and that I would work with him to get it.

I believe that 95 percent of meaningful communication is nonverbal and indirect, and that most of what mattered in that meeting was what I *didn't* say or do. To start, I didn't act like one of the hard-driving lawyers they had been fighting for the past nine months. I didn't lean on them to agree to a deal. Instead of pushing my needs, I offered them something: my interest and attention. I said, "I'm here to listen. Tell me everything I need to know."

Slowly Junior started to open up about his life. As he talked, I came to realize that for him, this negotiation had very little to do with money. The deeper challenges here were not legal complications or how to structure a deal. The issue was the relationship between Dale and his stepmother. A young man was stepping out on his own, away from the shadow of his parents, and he wanted respect and control of his own life. He had been the son of the famous driver, the stepson of the owner, the one everyone knew as "Junior," but now he wanted to feel acknowledged and treated well as his own man. That was what success meant to him.

Now I understood that those nine months of wrangling before I came on board and all those legal fees had been a waste. All the lawyers and the experts with their technical proposals had overlooked his deep motivation. But as we talked, Junior's tense body language started to relax. For the first time, he looked me in the eye. He said, "You're not what I expected." We were beginning to develop a relationship of trust.

I've seen it again and again. So many books on success and so many courses in business school promise to get you an edge so you can "beat" the other side, but in my experience, that's often the wrong goal. I've seen so many professionals—not to mention some family members—forget that the people across the table are still human beings. If those human beings don't have a relationship with you, or if they don't believe the relationship will bring them success, they won't do business with you. To win—and keep on winning—with them, you need to learn what success means, deep down, to them.

There was no quick fix for that contract negotiation or for that challenging family situation, but what we could change right away was the tone. We showed each other and the press that we were perfectly capable of continuing negotiations while also getting along and doing our jobs. Junior went back to concentrating on races and the media went back to reporting on them. Teresa and I focused on the work of making the company stronger and more successful. And although in time Junior felt he needed a break from the family and signed a contract with another team, we remained supportive of each other's efforts in the sport, continuing to build a relationship that I believe will bring the best outcome in the long term for everyone connected to the Earnhardt family.

A MORE POWERFUL WAY TO LISTEN

WHAT GOT ME PAST all the distractions to the heart of that negotiation with Junior was the way I listened. Most of the time, we tend to listen for whatever will help us prepare our next statement or make our next move. When I fall into that way of listening, you may be talking to me, but inside I'm focused on the goal or problem that's on my mind. I'm thinking about how to get what I want, and the truth is that I mostly tune you out—I listen to you just enough to find something I can use to form my next response, maybe even something in your words I can use against you. Of course, when I do this, you're going to feel that I'm not really there for you, not really listening, and you'll tend to pull away, back into your own agenda, just as I'm doing. That's why this first kind of listening tends to close people's minds and prolong their conflicts: each side keeps on going the way they were going all along.

But there is a second way of listening, which I think of as listening to understand. When we do that, we put aside our present problem for a little while and try to understand the larger situation of the person who's talking. That means listening not just for what they say, but what they mean—listening for what they need and care about, which often lies underneath their words. When you listen to understand me, I sense that I have your attention and your interest, and naturally I'll start to relax and get a little more comfortable. It's reassuring to have a respectful audience, to feel that my words aren't just a grab bag for you to dig around in and find something you can use. When you're listening to understand me, then I am freer to talk to you not just about what I planned to say, but about what matters most to me, what makes me tick.

It's an approach with a proven track record and a very long history. If you go all the way back to the life of Jesus, you'll notice that although he was a spiritual man, in Bible stories he's not usually found in the temple. You usually find him outside, meeting people in the regular paths of their life. His goal is to preach, but that's not what he does first. It's not even what he does second. He goes to where the people are and he listens to understand them. Once he's understood what they need, he responds to it. If they're hungry, he feeds them. If they're sick, he makes them well. Only after he both understands what they need and responds to their need does he start to preach.

In those Biblical stories, Jesus doesn't take this approach as a way to seem thoughtful or nice. He does it because listening to understand is the most effective way to reach the goal of spreading his message. I would say something similar is true in any kind of relationship, including business relationships, though the messages may be very different. So no matter what's on the table, I start by trying to step outside myself and listen for what the other person needs, their expressions of their deep motivation. Often it's not what I might expect, and it's rarely what they say up front. Usually people have some kind of surface style they wear for the situation—charming, confrontational, passive-aggressive, or whatever it may be—that mostly hides what moves them. Their words may not clarify things much either; I can count on one hand the times I've met a person who actually expressed precisely what he meant and what he needed from me. So when you get past the surface postures and the opening remarks, there's often a surprise waiting. Those surprises have made listening to understand the most eye-opening experiences of my life.

What I'm describing applies in every industry and every type of relationship, both business and personal. When I was newly married, I had some fixed ideas about what my wife, Jennifer, wanted from me and how I could make her happy. And she had some fixed ideas of her own. For a while, we just followed our fixed ideas and didn't listen to understand what the other wanted. The result was that two loving, committed newlyweds managed to kick up a whole lot of frustration and unhappiness.

For example, Jennifer thought that husbands wanted their dinners cooked when they came home from work, and though she had a demanding career of her own, she would put in the time to cook for us at night. I would come home and find her in the kitchen, but I wouldn't jump up and down with happiness and rave about her big dinner plans the way she expected. She felt offended and unappreciated, but I couldn't hear what she wanted, because I had my own ideas about what showed appreciation: Didn't I put money in the bank, bring home flowers or a new necklace now and then, and do other things she liked?

At first, when we tried to talk it out, we only listened for what would help each of us make our case: What do you mean you feel ignored? I spent two hours making your dinner! Or: How could you feel unappreciated? Didn't you see that necklace I brought home? It took us some time to start listening to understand. Finally I began to hear what mattered, deep down, to her. I told her, "I love a home-cooked meal, but we work so much that I would rather have two hours with you at night than to have you busy preparing the meal, then talk for a few minutes and go to sleep. I would rather go out to dinner or order in and have more quality time together." Along the way, she helped me to understand that while she appreciated flowers and other presents, what was even more important to her was that I sit with her on the back porch and talk with her, acknowledging her efforts, so she could see that I recognized the hard work she put into even small things she did for me.

Gradually we both learned to stop listening for what would help defend and justify what we had been doing and to start listening to understand what the other one needed. We came to see that it was unfair to make a decision about how to treat the other person if we didn't get good information first. You can call getting that information "being a good listener" or "ministering to souls in need" or "conducting effective market research." I don't really mind what you call it, because it all comes down to the same thing: listening to understand.

Of course, some people ask me, Max, is all this really necessary in business? If I have a simple business arrangement, do I still have to bother learning what makes them tick? My answer is that I don't think any business arrangement is simple. Maybe it seems that way sometimes to a customer who places a quick order, but that's only because the seller has done the work for the customer to make it *seem* easy. So if you're the one with goods or services to offer, or if you have a good professional connection with someone and you want to keep it that way, then you have a relationship to cultivate. And that means learning what makes the other person tick, whether he or she is your customer, your client, your boss, or your employee.

LISTENING LIKE A PRO

HOW DO YOU LISTEN to understand? To some people that might seem like the wrong question. Listening and talking are so basic, so everyday; do you really have to think about how to do them? I know I started off, years ago, with a very casual and intuitive approach to business conversation, and I did all right with it sometimes. But one of the things I learned from a career spent working with top performers, whether in music, sports, or business, is that almost anyone can give a great performance—now and then. Maybe one night with your friends you belt out a karaoke song and everyone tells you that you ought to be on *American Idol*. Well, you may have had a great night, but the question is, can you duplicate that performance the next time? And what about the time after that?

Professionals are professionals because they can perform over and over, in good conditions and bad, when they're feeling inspired and when they wish they could crawl back into bed. Even if communication comes naturally to you some of the time, it's worth getting clear just what it is you're doing right when you're at your best. Because the day will come when the stakes are higher or the conditions rougher, and you won't be able to cruise on instinct. You're going to need to be able to guide yourself—step-by-step like a great coach—through the challenge. So here are a few rules for listening to help others share what makes them tick when you first make contact. (Later I'll talk about going deeper, when you already have a relationship established.)

- **Show that you're interested.** As I said before, 95 percent of meaningful conversation is nonverbal and indirect—it's not the words you pick that get through to people. It's your body language: your tone of voice, your small actions and gestures. It's the physical things that show someone *you have my attention*:

Look them in the eye. Move slowly and calmly. Don't interrupt or take actions that pull the spotlight over to you; let it shine on them.

Put your cell phone and other distractions aside. Let them see that nothing interferes with your focus on them.

Let yourself respond, physically, to what they say. A laugh, a shrug, a raised eyebrow, or whatever comes naturally to you that lets them see they're not just talking, they're getting through. You don't have to put on a show for them, just let them see how you're affected by their words.

If you're speaking on the phone, avoid any distractions that they can hear—background noise or noise from a keyboard or electronic device. Let the other person know any time constraints you may have or any interruptions you anticipate, so they feel secure in their connection to you. Respond audibly to the important things they say, so they know you're with them.

- **Make them comfortable.** The main reason most people don't share what moves them is that they don't feel safe and respected. So often now our days are rushed and everyone has an agenda— I think many people feel, much of the time, either pressured or ignored, and neither one makes a person want to speak his or her heart. So start conversations gently. Make a joke, or if that's not your style, begin with any easy topic. At this early stage, everything you've heard about networking actually does apply. Pick a neutral, reassuring topic they can't get wrong—their favorite sport or hobby, their children or what they like to eat. What they'll notice won't be the topic, it will be the comfort they feel around you.

- **Delay your agenda.** Make clear that your interest is not just in achieving your own goals. In fact, put your goals on hold.

This was crucial in my first meeting with Junior, when more important than what I said to him was what I left out: no new proposals. No deal talk. No pressure to reach an agreement. By delaying conversation about my own agenda, I was showing him that I thought getting to know him was more important, for now, than anything. In the space I left, there was room for a relationship to begin.

- **Ask open-ended questions.** Don't make the mistake of limiting yourself to questions with a set response. If you ask about which team is going to win on Sunday or whether someone has kids, you're limiting the other person to set, factual responses. That tends to restrict a conversation. Open-ended questions get people started sharing their personal perspective, which is what you want them to do, but it still keeps things informal and comfortable. So instead of just complimenting that cute photo of their kids, you might ask, "It's a challenge, raising kids, isn't it?" Instead of just enthusing about a hobby or a team or their latest golf score, you might ask what they think about a well-known player or coach. Is this coach good for the team? It's a subtle shift, but once your open-ended questions make people feel comfortable telling you how they see little things, they'll ease into telling you bigger things. You'll be moving beyond ordinary networking into learning what makes people tick.

- **Watch for nonverbal signs of success.** How do you know this approach is working? Again, because much of communication is nonverbal, try to notice not just what they say but what they do. Do they seem more relaxed? (If you feel more relaxed, they probably do, too.) Are they talking more than at the start of the conversation? Are they willing to go beyond answering questions to offering observations and questions of their own? All of these are signs that you are gently breaking down the barriers to real communication, making it possible for them to share not just what they planned to say or what they usually say, but what matters to them.

- **Get ready for some surprises.** It's reassuring to go into a business conversation as prepared as you can be, but one thing many people forget to prepare for is surprise. In listening to understand, the whole point is to hear something you didn't know already about the other person's deep motivations. If you're fixed on your plan for the conversation, you may miss the unexpected opportunity that comes up. When I first met Junior, I didn't know that what mattered to him more than his contract negotiation was his family relationship. But as he talked, I heard it, and that was what made it possible for us to move forward.

ISN'T BUSINESS DIFFERENT?

A LOT OF PEOPLE tell me that they can imagine using this approach, listening to understand, in a social setting. If the objective is just to connect, to allow people to get to know each other, then sure, make them comfortable, listen to them, and see where the conversation goes. Find a common interest so you can get to know and like each other. If the other person opens up to you about a passion or a concern, then you have something more to talk about the next time, or something you can plan to do together to help the friendship deepen. There's really no agenda bigger than that, after all, in a social setting.

But in a business setting, or in social settings where people perceive networking opportunities, a lot of people assume this approach no longer applies. They do a little chitchat and then bang, out come the business cards and the business agendas. Soon—before they even know who they're dealing with—they're making their pitch. The problem here is that even when you're talking about straight business objectives, those objectives can only be reached by human beings, and human beings always have multiple agendas. They want to do well for their company, but also for themselves. They want to look great in their boss's eyes and in their lover's eyes and in the eyes of people you won't even know about, unless they tell you. They have passions they dream about and bills to pay and longer-term goals they work toward when they see the chance—a side project, a separate career track, or a hope for a different life. They have a past and something to prove about it. Business is never "just business." And if they don't let you know who you're talking to, your pitch to them may be way off base.

Take Stanley, a real estate broker I met socially who impressed me with his success in both up and down markets. In a casual conversation at a dinner party, he told me how much he had enjoyed a ball game he went to recently as the guest of a couple of bankers who approve mortgages. He mentioned that he encourages all of his clients to seek mortgages from this same team of bankers, and that those bankers take him to see a few games a year from some very nice seats. Now, imagine that I was a banker, too, and in this dinner chitchat I heard an opportunity to try to get Stanley to recommend my bank to his clients, instead of the one he had been using. Just from these remarks over dinner, I might have thought I knew what to do: if the guy loves baseball and he throws his business to the banker who gets him the good tickets, I could woo his business by offering something better (maybe playoff tickets?). But if I did that, I wouldn't be listening to understand—I would just be grabbing at one or two things he said to advance my own agenda.

As it happens, I'm not a banker and that night I had no agenda to push. I just kept talking with him, and I discovered that the story of his involvement with those bankers was more complicated. He had first met them through clients, and right away they hit it off. They talked about baseball and other topics, and he enjoyed it, but they weren't seeing any ball games together. He just enjoyed the small talk. Then one of his clients panicked about a deal that had seemed settled, but now was about to fall apart. Stanley was at a loss—he was very good at matching clients with homes in creative ways, but he had no special gift for reassuring them when they got scared. He told the bankers he was afraid they would lose the deal, and to his surprise they turned out to be very good at holding a client's hand and helping keep a deal from getting lost to panic. They talked the client down from the ledge and the deal was saved. Later Stanley had a drink with them, a little celebration, and that was the first time they proposed taking him to a game.

Hearing that story, I realized that it wasn't simply that Stanley liked bankers who got him tickets to ball games. As my understanding grew, I heard two other factors in play. The first was that he could relate to these particular bankers and enjoyed talking to them as people. The second was that he had an agenda of his own: he was good at finding clients and thinking outside the box about their housing needs, but not so good at the more psychological side of his job—the customer-care side. These particular bankers could help him meet that need, and they in turn appreciated the steady business Stanley provided, even in a down market, which more than made up for the extra work some of his clients required. Each of them was helping the other with a weakness. And the ball games weren't a payoff; they were a way to celebrate and deepen an existing relationship.

TECHNOLOGY MAKES LISTENING MATTER MORE

I KNOW IT MAY sound very old school, here in the twenty-first century, to focus so much on the power of one-on-one conversation, face to face, where people discover their shared interests and needs. Hasn't new technology changed the way we communicate? I would say sure, the technology has changed, but the technology that's succeeding is successful precisely because it helps us reach those same old deep, unchanging goals.

Take social networking sites. They are tremendously popular now, but why? It's because they're helping people get together with others who have the same passions, so they can connect with each other and do more of what they care about together. In fact, social networking sites like Facebook and Twitter are having far more success than advertising and other traditional forms of marketing for reaching young people. The research I've seen shows that while only 4 percent of teens now believe that ads tell the truth, 70 percent of teens visit social networks once a month. They don't trust advertising but they do trust their peers, and they make decisions based on the word-of-mouth validation they get from people with whom they have gotten comfortable and shared a common interest. So even at the cutting edge of marketing, people are still going through the age-old steps of sharing what makes them tick: they go into a chat room where they have a little more protection, a little more anonymity than they might have, face to face, and that protection helps them get comfortable and say more quickly what's really on their mind. The technology has changed, but at heart it still comes down to finding a place where people can share what makes them tick.

LISTENING TO UNDERSTAND OPPORTUNITY

MY WHOLE BUSINESS PHILOSOPHY is to discover how I can help other people look good, accomplish their goals, and feel right about their lives, and that always brings me back to listening to understand. That's why my first objective in a business setting, just as in a social setting, is to help the other person relax, so we can begin to develop a relationship of trust. Only then will that person feel right about sharing information about his or her needs, both personal and professional. Once I know who I'm talking to, then I can listen to understand what the opportunities are for us together, to help each other reach our goals. That's when I'm ready to do business.

But at the same time, all of our lives are busy and only getting busier. I can't sit around all day making other people comfortable and hoping they say something useful. That's why, over the years, I've worked up questions and research strategies, so I can go into each conversation prepared to learn what makes potential clients and customers tick as quickly as possible.

I start with personal research. If I know people who know the person I need to understand, I talk to those people. I read what I can in the press and on the Internet. As you would probably expect by now, my goal is not only to research the person's company or career path, but to get to know the whole person. Does this kind of research substitute for old-fashioned sitting and listening to what that person has to say? No, but it helps me anticipate areas in a conversation that I'll want to explore once we get comfortable.

In my background research and in my meetings with people, I rely on a list of questions I've developed over the years. These are not questions I ask directly, but questions I need to answer for myself to understand what makes them tick. Say I'm trying to understand someone named John. Here are some of the questions I might ask myself:

About John
- Do you know anything about John's family?
- Do you know his hobbies and interests?
- Have you ever had a discussion with John about life, love, and happiness?
- What motivates John besides love and money?
- What stands out in his accomplishments?

About John's work
- What do you know about his company's executives?
- What do you know about the challenges he faces?

- Do you know what frustrates him about his company? What he thinks the company does well, and what it doesn't do so well?
- Can you clearly state his strategic objectives, his company's objectives, and your objectives in dealing with him?

About John's future

- Where does John want to go with his company and with his own career goals in five years?
- How does what we offer, and the experience he'll have doing business with us, forward his own agenda?

That's a long list, and not every question is relevant every time. So let me make this clearer by giving an example of using such questions to create an opportunity—one I might otherwise have missed.

One major responsibility of the head of any sports team, apart from winning in competition, is to win new corporate sponsors and hold onto the ones you already have. I did this as president of DEI, and I continue to do it for NASCAR's Drive for Diversity program. Running a world-class team, no matter what the sport, has become extremely expensive, and my ability to give our drivers everything they need—from the best cars and garages to the best training and crews to the most comfortable travel and hotels so they can get a good night's sleep before each race—depends on sponsors. They provide not just money but also equipment and services, and in return we give them the opportunity to participate in our sport and to advertise to NASCAR fans, the most loyal fans in the world.

My challenge in pitching our team to sponsors is to find new ways that my team can stand out. Of course, all sponsors like to be associated with winners, and they like to put product logos and colors in front of as many people as they can. But there are many teams that boast winning drivers, and every team can offer a sponsor the chance to paint their logos and color schemes on a car, where it will be seen by millions at the track and on television. If many teams can offer similar things, then I have to push to find extra ways we can appeal to potential sponsors, something that makes us more competitive than the next team. That's where it becomes crucial to listen to understand the psychology of the people who speak for those potential sponsors, and do it quickly; we may only get one meeting to make our case.

I remember when I had the chance to pitch to a great potential sponsor for DEI, a company that had the resources to be a major supporter of our team and also provide the kind of positive image I wanted. I set up a meeting and learned that their representative would be a woman I had never met before, someone new to their organization. I didn't know anyone who knew her personally, but through research I was able to learn about her previous work background, which wasn't in racing but in telecommunications.

Once we started talking and had a chance to get comfortable, I started with an overview so I could watch her reactions. It was a deliberate attempt to find something she was passionate about. Some businesspeople who want to work with us are true fans of the sport, while others are feeling pressure from their finance committee to show a return on their investment. Some respond to a case-study approach and enjoy talking in economic terms. So as my team and I explained what we do and what we were looking for, we included as wide a range of our activities as we could.

At first, I got no special response. She seemed well informed about racing and sophisticated about her company's financial goals for the sponsorship, but neither subject seemed to hold any special excitement for her. Then I mentioned what was still a very new initiative, to reach out to fans through online digital and mobile-phone strategies. It was just getting started, and I wouldn't have mentioned it except that I had seen in my research that she had worked previously for a telecommunications firm. My research had suggested that cutting-edge communications might interest her, and sure enough, that was what got her attention. The whole tone of the meeting changed. She had been all business up to that point, but now she smiled. She said, "You're a man after my own heart." In her reaction and in the ideas she began to share, I saw that she had a passion for mobile phone campaigns. It became clear that this was something she would love to do, that she would do well, and that she felt would bring her the kind of attention she wanted at her own company. Had I not done my homework, we might never have discussed this passion of hers. But now we had identified an area of potential mutual benefit where her company's goals, my company's goals, and her own personal interests and career aspirations all came together. Now I had something to offer her that was unique. The point here is that people's interests have many levels, and you can't help them reach their goals until you begin to understand their deep motivations.

ESTABLISH TRUST AND DISCOVER WHAT MOVES PEOPLE

BE PROACTIVE ABOUT DISCOVERING the underlying agendas and personal interests that inform people's larger decisions.

- Once they are comfortable talking with you, listen for signs of what they prefer—what they would rather be talking about and doing.
- If you are newly establishing trust, try moving casually over topics across a range of your interests and activities. Watch for what gets them excited or talkative—that's a clue to what makes them tick.
- As the relationship starts to deepen, your questions should get more focused and specific.
- Once you have established real trust, you may even be able to ask directly: "What do you want from this? What's in this for you?"

Sometimes, no matter how well you research and listen, you find that you have no unique extra benefit to offer. There's nothing that gives you a decisive competitive advantage over other companies this person could work with or buy from. Even so, the basic principle of this chapter holds true: if this person has a choice, he will probably choose to do business with people he likes or with whom he feels an emotional investment. As personal agendas go, comfort, friendship, enjoyment, and loyalty are universal. Many of us spend the majority of our waking lives at work, and while we're there we would rather have a good time with good people. If you can offer the chance to make someone feel good about working with you, then you'll get chosen over those with similar objective qualities—and sometimes over those who look a lot better on paper.

So whether you are in a social setting or a business one, your objective is always to get people emotionally engaged with your program or your agenda *on a personal level*. The power of this principle blew me away when I was getting started in my career representing musicians. As an artist's representative, my goal was to help my artists not just to get the deal to make an album, but to have a success with that album. That meant getting the most support we could from the record company. There was a time when I assumed that an artist would go farthest if he or she could arrive with the music and approach as polished and ready for the market as possible. It seemed logical that if we showed up with the songs written, the arrangements perfected, the demo recorded, and the sequence of songs—even the title and concept for the album—all ready to go, then we would be making the record company's job easier and they would get behind us for that reason. But what I discovered instead was that people like to feel emotionally invested. If a producer could bring in his own cowriter to help write a new song, or a new musician to play on it, or contribute ideas for the arrangement, then that producer was likely to feel the song was partly "his," and he would care more about it and give far more of his energy and his time to helping it succeed than if it arrived basically ready to go. Again and again, I found that when my artists accepted help, whether it was changing a title or reconsidering their audience and how to reach it, accepting a visual concept for the album cover from the art department or a marketing concept from the publicists, we found that the pride and the commitment the professionals at the record company felt for the artist's work escalated tremendously, and we got far more support and resources than if we had made it "easier" for them by doing it all ourselves. I learned that what people respond to, even more than having someone make their job easy, is to feel emotionally engaged.

LISTENING TO UNDERSTAND CRISIS

AS POWERFUL AS IT can be to listen to understand when looking for potential opportunities, it's just as powerful when you're in a crisis. For me, it has made a big difference in handling some of the most challenging professional situations I have faced. I'm thinking now of what was probably the worst single meeting in my life, a crisis that hit me almost completely by surprise.

One day I got a letter out of the blue from someone representing one of DEI's long-standing corporate sponsors. The relationship went back to long before I was hired, and the benefits for us included a seven-figure payment every year, plus another seven figures worth of equipment that we used in our racing operation. We had two years left in our contract with the sponsor when a letter arrived saying that the sponsor needed me to fly to their corporate headquarters for a meeting as soon as possible. Now, this was definitely out of the ordinary.

I called up the representative who had written the letter, and his words sounded very friendly. He told me we had lots of friends in common, that he had heard a lot of good things about me, and so forth, but that the sponsor wanted to talk to me. I said that before I took the meeting, I needed to know the agenda so I could come prepared. Again, he gave me a warm-sounding response, but he remained vague—they wanted "a working meeting," he said. They wanted to "look into a couple of things in the contract, talk about some valuation issues." He told me, "I'm a guy who likes win-win situations." He sounded positive, but his words were empty. So here already was a conflict between his words and his nonverbal cues. It was a sign that something wasn't right, but I couldn't get much useful information from him. The one thing I did learn was that since our last meeting, the sponsor had undergone a complete change of management. The president was new, as was the global head of marketing, the head of the motorsports division, and so on. When we got off the phone, I researched our recent dealings with the sponsor a little further. I reviewed our previous contacts. I also learned that they were late with a check they owed us for $750,000. On the appointed day my management team and I flew to their headquarters.

The sponsor was a manufacturing company. I always like to show my respect for the differing cultures of the companies we deal with, so my team arrived dressed appropriately for the occasion, we thought, in slacks and shirts. Their entire new management team was waiting for us, along with the representative who had written to me, and they were all in business suits. That's when I knew it was an ambush.

The representative who had contacted me did all the talking. He told us how frustrated they were with our company. He said they had done a valuation of what they had been paying us in the sponsorship deal, and that what they had received wasn't worth close to what they paid. He told us that we were unresponsive and impossible to deal with, and that they felt frustrated and personally slighted. This relationship was over, he said. There would be no further payments or deliveries from them, and in fact by their calculations we owed them $1.5 million. Then he turned around and said we shouldn't take any of this personally. It was a business decision, and he wanted to walk us through their analysis of the value we had failed to provide so we could see for ourselves why they alleged we were in breach of contract.

My general counsel was with me, and he said, "All right, let's see this analysis of yours." But I said, "No. Stop." Because as clear as this representative's words might have been, the nonverbal cues in the room—the most important parts of the communication—were telling a different story. Until now, this representative had done all the talking, and everything he said had been to set us up so they could get out of their contract. But there were four other people across the table, the actual management team for our sponsor, and none of them had said a thing. The president of the company, in particular, was sitting there in his suit closed up tight, looking very uncomfortable. He didn't look like a man who was getting what he wanted. His body language told me that in some way, he didn't like what he was hearing. Even though he was letting this other guy represent him, he wanted to talk. I thought if I could provide an opening for him to speak I could learn what it was he wanted. In short, to change the conversation I had to get past the representative and somehow reach the uncomfortable man in charge.

I started to push and to prod, almost like I was a lawyer cross-examining a witness, to see if I could get him talking so that he would say something that would help me understand what I needed to do to save the relationship. Was I sure he wanted to save it? No. But this was my chance to try.

I said, "First of all, I *am* taking this personally. I asked for an agenda for this meeting and I was given nothing, and now I feel ambushed. I take complete offense." Now everyone looked uncomfortable. No one likes to be told to their face that their business practices are unprofessional and offensive. "Quite frankly," I went on, "this is the first time I've heard anything about difficulty in this relationship from my management team. We take a lot of pride in all our relationships and what we do for our sponsors. This is no way to do business. I want to know what's beneath this." I kept going, criticizing their handling of the business relationship, until finally their president exploded. "We don't even have a relationship!" he said.

If I had flown off the handle then, or gotten pulled into a legal back-and-forth about their metrics and their valuation of our deal, then we all could have left angry, and that would probably have been the end of that long and valuable partnership. But there was another option here, now that he was talking—the option to start a conversation and show him I was concerned about his needs. I said, "With all due respect, sir, you've been with your company for fourteen months, and I've been in my job for sixteen months. I agree that you and I don't have a relationship, but that's because your team hasn't made the necessary effort. With every other commercial partner I have, I can tell you with great specificity what their objectives are with their sponsorship. I can tell you a lot about them personally. But you fired your previous director of motorsports, and I've never even had a conversation with your new man or with you. We haven't had the chance to have a relationship."

Then his representative began to get smart with me. He said, "You ought to know how these sponsorship things work. It's up to you to notify the sponsor of any changes in your organization or in marketing programs that impact their investment."

I didn't let the representative's criticism distract me. By now I had heard that the president of the company was willing to talk about the relationship, and so I just kept talking to him and his management team. I said, "Hold on, time out." Turning to their new director of motorsports, I said, "When you started your job, you contacted me, and I gave you my personal cell number and made myself available to you. But when I got my team ready to meet, your guys cancelled the meeting. You've cancelled three meetings in a row."

He hadn't spoken yet. Now he said, "You're absolutely right."

Then I said, "Second of all, I'm all about protocol and respect. If you're the one managing this, what does it make me look like if I go around you to your president? He's entrusted it to you to lead on this, so I have to respect his choice and wait on you."

I could see I had their attention. They were acknowledging that I had been trying to meet their needs and treat them with the respect that they deserved. I was speaking the language they valued, the language of committed, professional managers.

Now, as they calmed down enough to listen a little, and I could feel everyone in the room start to get more comfortable, I worked to show them my interest in understanding their needs and becoming the kind of business partner they wanted most. I began asking open-ended questions. What were they trying to achieve with their brand? What were the president's objectives? What financial pressures were they under? I tried to talk to them thoughtfully about every type of concern that I know is important to managers, focusing on their needs, as if I had no agenda but their success. Even in that ambush situation, I was delaying my own agenda—I didn't say anything about what we needed from them or what action we would take if they backed out on us. I kept talking until the tone had changed completely.

When the meeting was over, the representative who had first contacted me walked us out of the office. He said, "You know, they told me to give you two options, and that either way they were getting out of this contract. But you turned the whole meeting around."

Soon after, I received an e-mail from their vice president of marketing. It said, "Although it wasn't the best of circumstances, the information exchange we had today was very, very productive. We look forward to continuing the conversation."

Immediately I had my general counsel send an e-mail saying that we appreciated the meeting and that we were a loyal company that valued our long relationship with them. We said we would bend over backwards to be great partners, and that maybe even, as a great partner, we would go out and look for someone to relieve them of their obligations to us. But while we were doing all this, they needed to understand that we had a deal for two more years, and we fully expected them to pay us.

Soon the representative called me, saying, "No, no, no, you don't have to replace us. I think we can salvage this." He had specific mar-

keting ideas he wanted to talk about. We were back in business together, and the multimillion-dollar relationship was restored, because
I had been able to hear in what the president of the company said—
and most important, at first, in what he didn't say—that there was
still a basis for a business relationship. By listening to understand, we
moved beyond the crisis to a profitable understanding of what made
them tick.

CHAPTER TWO

See **Where** You **Want** to Be,
Not **Where** You **Are**

I MEET SO MANY talented people, and visit so many well-regarded organizations, yet I find that many have lost their most crucial connection: the connection to where they want to be next. Instead of focusing on their future, they get stuck on where they are now or where they've been. If they've done well, they grow complacent—looking in the mirror of other people's admiration and attention, resting on past accomplishments, relying on reputation instead of dedication. Or, if they're not where they want to be, they complain. They analyze. They regret. Maybe they feel like it's hopeless, like there's nowhere better to go. It happens to young people who can't see a way clear to the future; it happens to stars and whole organizations at the top of their game; it happens to all of us sometimes—we get distracted from that essential focus on getting where we want to be. Yesterday you may have had a win or a loss, but to me, it almost doesn't matter. Either way, if you're stuck on the *then* or the *now*, you're no longer seeing where you want to be.

Think about it. Most of us grew up hearing the reminder, "Keep your eye on the ball." We studied our great leaders, and heard how they kept their eyes on the prize. And yet too often we find, if we're honest, that we've focused all our attention and energy on the ground right under our feet. It's as if we've taken the trouble to check our location on a map, and we've found that little circle marked "you are here," and then we just stand there and stare at it. Why is that so wrong? Where you are now, *wherever it is,* has been achieved. You've done it—or maybe it's been done to you—but whether it's good, bad, or some of both, focusing on it only keeps you there. So if you aspire to go anywhere else, to be anything more, you need to look away from your present circumstances and focus on the future that inspires and energizes you. It's as true of organizations as it is of individuals, as true of business matters as spiritual ones. Lift your eyes up. See where you want to be.

GOALS AND PLANS ARE NOT ENOUGH

MAYBE YOU THINK YOU know what I'm going to say next. Maybe it sounds like I'm going to talk about setting yourself some goals and then following them, step-by-step like rocks across a stream, until you get to the other side. No. A lot of people take time to list their goals and draft their business plans, and sometimes I'm one of them, but I've learned that while lists and plans can be useful, the big successes in my life haven't come from mapping out a path and following it step-by-step or goal by goal. Sure, I've made a lot of plans along the way, from personal plans to formal business plans, and I've been blessed with some great successes. But the truth is that none of my successes ever went according to plan—at least not according to any plan of mine. And when I've had a success that felt bigger than I ever dreamed possible, and I've started to think, "Now I've got it, now I know how it's done," I've found out soon enough that there was still more to do and a whole lot more to learn about doing it.

Here's the thing about plans, whether we're talking about personal goals or formal business plans for major ventures: plans change. You can map out your road to success, step-by-step, but maps have a way of going out of date, or turning out to be plain wrong. When Columbus set out in 1492, he had the best maps he could buy with the King of Spain's money and a clear goal: to find a new trade route to bring spices back from India. And how did it turn out? Columbus blew it. He never got to India. He never even got close to his objective. He tried calling the unfamiliar people he met on his travels "Indians," but that didn't change the truth. Yet although he never achieved his goal, he achieved something bigger. He wanted to be a great explorer and give Spain a new, prosperous trade route, and he did; it just didn't come according to plan.

I wouldn't call myself a Columbus, but I do see now that my whole career grew from keeping my eyes on a future I didn't know, practically, how to reach: starting a talent agency to represent sports and entertainment figures. Of course, today, if you look over my resume, that might sound like it was a natural way for me to go. After all, if my goals back then were to run record companies and sports organizations, why not start out by representing artists and athletes? That way I could develop my practical experience in both sports and entertainment, so that when sports organizations needed to evolve to become more like entertainment companies (I'll say more about that later on), I could combine my experience on the sports side and the entertainment side and make it work. It sounds great now, doesn't it? But that's only with hindsight. Those weren't my goals, back then. I didn't know how sports organizations were going to evolve. I had no master plan. I was just a law student who dreamed about being a talent agent, and even when it came to that, I didn't know what I was doing. I might as well have been trying to pull a career out of a magician's hat.

I want to tell you how it happened, so you can hear just how much I *didn't* have planned, how important it was that I didn't limit myself to fixed goals—and what powerful results came, instead, from *seeing where I wanted to be*. The story begins when I was still in law school, rooming with my friend, Mickey Carter. One day we decided to go into business together. How did we do it? First, we made up a name for our business by combining his name with mine. Then we shook hands; that was our contract. Now, we felt, it was official. We went to

Kinko's and had business cards printed, we bought a cheap thermal fax machine that we hooked up to the phone line in our room, and we went to the post office and got a mailbox for our business correspondence, just in case anyone ever sent us a letter. That was it. We were still students, we weren't licensed, we had no money, but we could see where we wanted to be: discovering hot new talent and managing emerging artists.

Now we needed clients. How did a company get clients? Referrals, right? We needed some contacts in the business to refer potential clients our way. Did we have any contacts? Just one—my sister, Traci, who was working for a gospel radio station in Charlotte, North Carolina. Traci knew where we wanted to be, and one day she called to say that a singer named John P. Kee was having success with his choir, traveling quite a bit and growing an audience, especially among young people. At the time, there were a lot of older gospel performers who tended to appeal to an older audience. John appealed to youth as well. As we soon discovered, young African-American kids were attending his shows, rushing up to the stage, some of them crying as they sang John's lyrics along with him and his awesome choir. It seemed he might be finding a way to make gospel music cool, to attract a whole new generation, but Traci said he needed help managing the business side. Mickey and I decided to cut classes and drive down to Charlotte to meet him. These were our goals: to get a meeting with him, pitch to him all the ways we could be useful to his business, and sign him as a client.

Now, neither of the cars we owned back then would have survived the twelve-hour trip from Indiana to North Carolina, so we pooled our money for a rental and drove down to see him. As soon as we got in the room with John, we started telling him all the things we could do for him, from returning his business calls and answering his mail up to more important matters. We had been making our pitch for about fifteen minutes when he interrupted and said he had to go. He had to play in a charity basketball game. Could we talk some other time?

Well, we hadn't driven all of that way for a fifteen-minute meet-ing, so we asked him, "Can we play basketball with you?" He seemed a little surprised, but he said sure. So Mickey and I drove to a sporting goods store and bought gym shoes, tube socks, shorts, and shirts, and we played ball with John and some of his choir members. John P. Kee, the future breakthrough gospel star, became our first client—and we became actual talent agents.

What made the difference here? It was a big help to have Traci as our connection at the gospel radio station, to recognize the talent and promise in John and to provide the referral for us, but referrals are no guarantee of anything. Lots of referrals go nowhere. And certainly my close friendship with Mickey was important as we started our busi-ness, but plenty of friends share dreams that never become reality. So what was it? I believe the secret to our success was the way Mickey and I helped each other to ignore our unimpressive present situation—no clients, no license, no experience, no office—and to focus instead on seeing the future we wanted. We were ready with our business cards, and more than that, we had plenty of time to talk about the business we wanted to run. When we got our fifteen minutes with John, we knew what we wanted to say. Most important, we felt a commitment to the future we wanted. We could see it out there ahead of us, and we were prepared to jump toward it when we got the chance—even if we had to do it on a basketball court.

Looking back, it was a good use of the principle *know what makes them tick* to play in a charity ball game with our future star client. It showed him how much we had in common, and just how committed we were both to having a relationship with him and to the larger val-ues of the gospel community, which were the values that made John tick. It showed our creativity and our enthusiasm for this work. But to be honest, that's just hindsight talking. We had no goal on our list that said, "Establish personal relationship with Kee through social/ charitable activity." Our goal was just to pitch to him on the practical business services we could offer, and that's what we did. Once he got up to go, we improvised the rest because we were afraid that if we let him out of our sight, we would never hear from him again. So let me repeat this point, because it matters so much: while it can be useful to list your goals and draft your plans, it's never enough. Plans change. *It's your motivation that needs to stay consistent.*

DANGER: FIXED GOALS

NOW I'LL GO EVEN further. I'm not just saying that writing down goals and then crossing them off your list isn't enough to build success. I'm saying that the way a lot of people set goals actually *threatens* their success. And that's true whether you're a rookie or seasoned pro. If you're green, like Mickey and I were when we first drove down to Charlotte for that meeting, you just don't have the experience to imagine all the steps that will take you from where you are to where you want to go. You shouldn't tie down your future self to the plans written by your clueless past self. You should be able to accommodate smart changes. If Mickey and I had stuck to our original plan—if we had just given our business pitch and waited for an answer—we might still be waiting.

But even if you're an old pro, it's still dangerous to be too wedded to a plan, because you may feel so comfortable working in the ways you've anticipated—or the ways that have worked for you before—that you miss the opportunities no one can see coming, which can be the biggest opportunities of all. The problem with setting concrete, specific goals is that reaching success is always an unpredictable process, and it's the process, not the goals, that get you where you want to be.

This is all the more true in a time of accelerating change and an increasingly diverse global marketplace where people do business with people from all sorts of backgrounds and from all over the world. Technological change is moving so fast that the computers in science-fiction movies look old-fashioned just a few years later. Your vision of where you should be nine steps from now may soon be as out of date as that guy in the big flashing robot suit on *Lost in Space*. Remember him? Better to focus on taking the next step.

I know a woman who became the top female executive in one of the biggest insurance companies in the world. She did it in part because of her early encouragement from her father, who believed a woman should be able to have a career if she wanted one. In fact, when it became clear to him that his teenage daughter had work ambitions, he personally offered to help her set goals. He introduced her to three women who had themselves succeeded in their work. They were:

- A nurse
- A schoolteacher
- The proprietor of a Laundromat

Now, he wasn't wrong—I believe his daughter could have done well working any one of those jobs—but the *goals* he could imagine for her were much too limiting for someone of her talents and opportunities. In time, she found that she needed to put aside the specific goals he had offered, and instead hold on to his bigger lesson: that if there's a job you want, it's useful to meet people like you who've done that job. Taking that approach, she left her hometown to work in Washington, D.C., and then New York, where she found mentors and role models beyond what she had ever known and success in a career her family barely understood until she explained it to them.

I love personal examples, and especially stories of people just starting out or bouncing back from hard times, because anyone can feel the urgency and relate to them. But I would be wrong if I gave the impression that what I'm saying only holds for individuals. The fact is, setting fixed goals can be just as limiting when you're dealing with whole organizations and industries. I found that what was true when I was just starting out representing recording artists still held true when

I had the chance to be part of the biggest deal in the history of gospel music. This deal changed the whole music industry, with effects we're still feeling to this day, but if I had stuck to my goals and the plans I went in with, this game-changing deal could never have happened.

The chance came after we had represented John P. Kee for several years. By then he had made good on his promise, becoming the most successful gospel artist on Tyscot Records, the largest and oldest independently owned black gospel label. John's albums had charted higher and higher until he hit number one on the gospel charts with "We Walk by Faith." But back then, the whole gospel industry still ran on a mom-and-pop basis. The albums were sold in small stores that were serviced by a limited distributor, and even a big gospel artist only sold forty or fifty thousand albums—not much compared to big pop and R&B successes that "went platinum" with sales of a million copies.

Artists got involved with gospel music back then almost exclusively for the sake of the ministry—to help usher people into the presence of God. Their devotion was something I could understand: I had seen how in our churches, just like in so many houses of worship for faiths around the world, what moved people and readied them for the religious message was music. But I also saw that with gospel people so focused on ministry, no one seemed to be considering gospel's *business* possibilities. I knew there were a lot more people out there who would enjoy and benefit from this powerful, healing music, and that what prevented this was small marketing budgets and limited distribution. Little independent companies like Tyscot couldn't always afford to put enough records into stores when their artists were getting good publicity, so potential fans went looking for the music they had heard about and were turned away. Other times, there was no money to publicize the good records that were waiting on the shelves. So when John's contract ran out and it was time to renegotiate with Tyscot, I went in very aggressively. I said, look, he's already your biggest artist, and he has tremendous potential. You need to commit more resources to marketing and distributing his albums. I laid out my ideas, and my recollection is that I blew them away with what I had in mind. They asked for some time to think it over.

While they were doing their thinking, their distributor went bankrupt. Let me explain what this meant for us exactly, because it's one reason why we had the chance to change the way the whole game was played. When an artist made an album, the record company paid to have it recorded and to have the physical recording—the record or CD—created. So Tyscot put up the money for John's album. Then a separate company, the distributor, shipped the album to the stores. They collected the money that the stores made from customers, and paid the record company, usually once every three or four months. When the distributor went broke, it couldn't pay Tyscot anything, even though some of their records were selling well. So now my client's record company was broke. They couldn't pay their artists. They couldn't even pay their bills. There was no way they could pay for the big new marketing plan I had in mind. I thought, what do we do now? It's not going to work the old way. It was time to break the mold and try something new.

My partner Mickey and I sat down with the owner and the president of Tyscot in a hotel room. It was a stressful moment for all of us. Not only was John our biggest client, but this was my first big deal, the biggest transaction of my career so far—not just financially, but because it could prove what type of businessman I was. No one knew me yet on a national scale, or saw what I believed I was capable of doing. This was my chance to make a name for myself as credible, knowledgeable, and effective—it was like being put into a playoff game as a pinch hitter. I had one shot to show what I could do in the national spotlight.

Meanwhile, in the eyes of Tyscot, I was the enemy. As Minister Bryant Scott, the president of the company, will tell you, they assumed my plan was to hit them when they were down, to steal away their top earner when the company needed him most. And this much was true: I had an intuition by then that the way to get John's music a much wider audience was to go beyond working with the limited resources of gospel companies, and to use the broader commercial music industry instead. In particular, I had a strong feeling that I could take John to Zomba Label Group, a division of Sony/BMG that had recently signed another traditional gospel artist we represented, Vanessa Bell Armstrong, to Jive, their pop/R&B/hip-hop label. I knew it would be very different, of course, working with a big, secular, mostly white record company, but I was young and naïve enough to think I could make it work.

As we sat across the table at that tense meeting, my goal seemed obvious to everyone: I was John's representative, so my job was to get him the most money and the best distribution I could, no matter who I had to push aside to do it. They were fully expecting me to tell them, sorry, but you're a little company, and now you're broke and in breach of contract. My guy is going to be a big star with a big, commercial company, so thanks for building him up when he was small—we'll see you later.

That goal made some obvious sense: if we could cut out Tyscot and work directly with a big company like Sony/BMG, then we would get better marketing and distribution for John's albums, plus more money up front and no need to share that money with anyone else. In terms of the bottom line, cutting out the little man seemed the obvious way to go. It was what agents did when they got the chance. It was what management consultants did when they were brought into a struggling company. On paper, it made all the sense in the world.

But the obvious right move didn't feel so right to me. I could see already that it made John uncomfortable. Sure, he wanted to get into a bigger distribution system with more financial stability, which could mean a better chance to reach more souls; but that commercial system had no understanding or respect for ministry. They were just interested in selling albums. Working with a big, commercial company might make it harder to reach the people who wanted it most, the existing gospel audience, who relied on the small companies to bring them ministers with real integrity.

So when I sat down across the table from Bryant Scott and his father, Dr. Leonard Scott, I didn't hand them their walking papers. I took some time to find out what made them tick. I asked why they had gotten into the gospel music business in the first place. And they started talk to me not about business, but about their passion for ministry. They talked about their dream that the artists they worked with, who felt such a calling to spread the Word, would be able to turn that calling into a true vocation and make a life out of it, a life in which they could still pay their rent and support their families. I learned that this wasn't just a nice idea to them: they had invested their own money in the business. And they were committed to their artists— they made clear right up front that they were willing to let John go to another company if that was what it took for him to grow as an artist. This went against their own business goals, but I was learning that what made them tick was a deep integrity that counted for more than short-term profits. That integrity seemed to explain something else they told me: many of their other artists were signing up with them again, even though they couldn't guarantee when the company would be able to pay them. For them, I was coming to understand, gospel music was a long-term commitment, and they viewed their artists as true partners in an enterprise that was as much about doing good as it was about doing well.

That spoke to me. By this time, I represented not just gospel musicians but also R&B and hip-hop groups as well. Our firm had grown to thirty employees. While there were some great artists among my clients, many were connecting to their audience through the scummiest parts of human nature—violence, drug abuse, and exploitative sex. But gospel music had helped bring on the more peaceful times in my own family, and it had helped many others find a reason to go on living. For me, personally, that was where I wanted to be, not helping to spread the word about the "bitches and hos" of hip-hop.

The more we talked, and the more I came to understand what made Bryant and Dr. Scott and the people at Tyscot tick, the more the tone of our negotiation changed. I realized that while we were all feeling stress in that hotel room over the bankruptcy of our distributor, we weren't enemies. Yes, we were on different sides of this current problem, but that was only where we were now. If we looked instead at where we all wanted to be, it was the same place. We wanted to find success with this music that had saved and enriched so many people's lives. We wanted John to have the chance to grow as an artist, to make his amazing records and spread his message of integrity. And so I asked myself, how can we work this out together?

As an agent, the short-term goal is always to get your client as much money as possible up front. You don't know what the future will bring, so you take as much as you can get, right now. But I also knew artists. I spent a lot of my time in the recording studio and talked with songwriters when they were blocked or unsatisfied with the quality of their new songs. I knew that to do great creative work, an artist has to be comfortable. At Tyscot Records, John had people who understood him as an artist better than anyone. They knew who he was, how to settle him down when he was upset, and how to encourage his best work. When his trust was shaken or when he was angry, they could help him get back to the right space to give a performance or go back into the studio. They kept him in his comfort zone, and that was huge.

They also knew how to connect with his core audience. They had relationships with the churches and the gospel radio announcers who played his records and spread the news about fresh releases. The company had a reputation with the fans: as the largest, oldest, independently owned black gospel label, they had credibility. If Tyscot was behind an artist, that validated the album.

So as we sat across the table in that hotel room, I told them, let's not fight each other. Let's turn this into a partnership. Your goal may have been to keep John at your company. My goal may have been to get John the biggest commercial deal we could get. But together we can do something bigger than what any of us could do on our own.

I went back to Clive Calder, who was Zomba's owner, and Barry

Weiss, the company's president who had signed Vanessa Bell Armstrong to the Jive label. Historically, they had artists like DJ Jazzy Jeff and the Fresh Prince, KRS-One Boogie Down Productions, and also pop artists like Backstreet Boys and, later on, Britney Spears. They had hip-hop artists like Too $hort, whose adult lyrics couldn't be played on pop radio. They had a lot of talent but no one taking anything like the approach that John was taking. Clive wanted John P. Kee because he recognized a fantastic talent, but the truth was that John didn't fit there. I said to Barry: we want to work with you but Jive's brand won't resonate with gospel people. In fact, it wasn't working for Vanessa Bell Armstrong, either. She had gotten a good deal and a big pop-star launch in the mainstream style, but the church community had rejected it. There was backlash against her in the gospel music press. She wasn't getting booked for as many concerts. Sales were poor.

I told the decision makers at Zomba: it's not enough to take a gospel artist, no matter how great, and plug in your usual hit-making formula. You can't sign John to Jive. To have credibility with the gospel music consumer, you need a gospel company that gets what the music and the ministry is all about. If you can start a gospel label, we can bring both of these artists to the new label, with Tyscot as a creative partner and a joint venture partner in John's records.

I knew it would mean thinner profit margins for all of us, since we would have to share the income from John's albums among Zomba, Tyscot, and ourselves, but with more commercial resources and a better distribution system, and the deal structured to represent everyone's interests, I hoped we would sell more records and make up the difference that way. And sure enough, John P. Kee's next album, *Show Up*, didn't sell forty or fifty thousand records. It sold six hundred thousand. For the first time, a black gospel artist was having success like a pop or hip-hop star. And it was possible because we didn't limit ourselves to the goals we had in mind when we sat down together. We put our specific goals and plans aside and kept our sights not on where we were, but on where we wanted to be.

YOU DON'T NEED A MASTER PLAN

I'VE HEARD SOME OF the people I've worked with over the years say, "Oh Max, he's always got a master plan," as if somehow I have all the steps worked out in advance. That's flattering in a way, but the truth is that it only looks like a master plan in hindsight. Almost any series of moves, whether in business or on a race track or on a basketball court, *looks* logical and well planned if it ends in success— but that doesn't necessarily mean it was planned out. It just means it worked. If I'm dribbling down court and I fake left and go right, pass to a teammate then turn around, catch a return pass, and score, it's going to look to a lot of people in the stands like a well-planned play. And maybe I did have it all planned out. But maybe I threw that pass to my teammate because I was hung up, and getting rid of the ball was simply the best I could do at the time. Then an opportunity opens up that hadn't been there a few seconds before. If I grasp that opportunity and score, I may look like I knew what I was doing every minute, and the fans may never know that I was just playing my best, from one moment to the next, and keeping an eye on where I wanted to be.

WHAT VISION REALLY MEANS

SO WHAT DOES BRING success after success, if planning alone can't do it? Some people would say that if you can "see" where you want to be, and if seeing that possible future keeps you motivated to reach it, then God has given you a vision. I think "vision" is a fine word, but it can be confusing, even intimidating. It sounds like something that only certain rare individuals can have, but that's not right. Here's what people don't always get about vision: to find your vision, you don't need to do anything rare or fancy. You don't have to climb the mountaintop. You don't have to hear angels sing. All "vision" means is having your own mental picture that moves you, some practical desire that will make you feel better about your life when you get it, because it's part of what makes you tick.

It can be very simple. As a teenager in the Indianapolis ghetto, my vision was just this: to go to school, with decent shoes that fit my feet and clothes that weren't so obviously secondhand or pulled out of the irregular bin at the back of some discount store that I was embarrassed to wear them. My family was poor; I didn't always have the kind of clothes that kids from other families had, and the trouble was, people made assumptions. Even now there are a few families back in Indianapolis who would be happy to tell you all about how they knew Max Siegel back in the day. But if you talk with them, they probably won't mention that when I came to their doors to ask their kids to come out and play, they didn't invite me in. They made me wait outside, because I wasn't dressed like the kind of child they wanted in their house.

Then there was the doctor at the hospital where my mother worked as a nurse, an African-American like us. My mother asked him a favor: would he talk to me about what it took to become a doctor? Would he let me follow him around the hospital one day and get a feel for whether that could be the right career for me? He said yes, but when he met me and got a look at my secondhand clothes, and he learned that I went to a public school in the ghetto, he told me: you're already at a disadvantage. You don't have what it takes to be a professional. *Don't bother.*

So as a teenager my vision was that one day people would stop judging me based on how I looked or where I lived and went to school. I started with what I could control most easily: my clothes. Back in the day, the look was "preppy." That meant Ralph Lauren shirts with the little Polo insignia on the chest. Designer jeans. Argyle socks. This was expensive stuff, as far as I was concerned. I got a job working as a cook at Long John Silver's, and when I got paid I took my money to a store called the Cash Bargain Center. They sold authentic brands, but with defects. I hunted and hunted through those bins, looking for a shirt with a defective seam you wouldn't really notice. I kept looking until I found something acceptable.

The kids from those more solid families had an expression you heard around school sometimes: they said "always dress for your next step." And when I got some new clothes and shoes, I looked a little less like the kid who got asked to stand outside, and a little more like one of those kids who would make something of himself. Those little successes kept me going. I had no master plan, or at least no master plan that led where I planned (I never did become a doctor). But I could see where I wanted to be, living a better and more reliable life, and I was feeding my own deep motivation, day after day, to get there. I took each step as well as I could. To start, I was looking more like the kids from the families where the parents had better jobs, the families that could afford to take a vacation together once a year, that didn't have to keep moving because they couldn't afford their house. I remember going to work at that restaurant kitchen, thinking it would sure be nice not to come home and see a moving van: my vision was for a more stable life. It was enough.

Because mentoring is very important to me, I always want to be sure that the suggestions I share are the real thing. The power of "seeing where you want to be" was confirmed for me not long ago when I had the chance to talk with my high school principal, Don King, for the first time in many years. Back when I was a student, he believed in my potential and helped by recommending me to Notre Dame. (I often returned the favor, hosting students from my area and elsewhere so they could visit Notre Dame and encouraging them to come.) But after I went to law school, Mr. King and I lost touch, and when I saw him again years later he hadn't heard where my career had taken me. Here was a chance to test out one of my principles. What had I been like back then, when it all got started? Mr. King remembered me as a good athlete and as a member of the student government. He remembered that I took the most challenging academic classes available. He also remembered me as "persistent, polite, and well dressed," so I guess those clothes made a difference. But he had no idea what I had done with my life, and no real guesses. In an interview, he said this: "I would visit an academic class and there was Max, taking all the right courses to prepare himself for the future, but I don't think he had any idea what it would be." Hearing him say that, I felt even more certain of how far a person or a team or a whole company can go, plan or no plan, experience or no experience, if they can see where they want to be.

DISCOVER YOUR VISION

SO HOW DO YOU do it? How do you find that vision of where you want to be that's practical enough to keep you moving, day after day? By getting back to basics: *know what makes them tick.* By "them" what I really mean is . . . you. To discover your vision—or to rediscover it if you've gotten distracted—you need to listen to understand, as I described in chapter 1, but the person you need to understand is yourself. You need to recognize that you are your most important client, the ally who is going to make it all possible, and the one you must take care of at all costs.

Think of it as a partnership between you and your future self. Just like any other partnership, you two need to get to know each other, find your shared needs, and work together to satisfy them. The same rules apply. You may ask, is your future self really enough of a "person" to partner with? What could a "future self" need when it doesn't even exist? Well, that is a good place to start: your future self needs to exist. It can't do it without you. It needs you to bring it into being. You need it, too—you need the promise of that future when you attain the success that matters most to you. You need the reassurance that it's worth doing your best, today, and that you're not crazy to try. That's what my first partner, Mickey Carter, and I had before we ever had a client for our talent agency: a connection we could feel to our future, successful selves.

The fact is, most people have a little success, but either they can't build on it when they get the chance or they can't appreciate what they've got, and soon it slips away. You need the focus and the commitment that comes from feeling that your future self is out there, waiting for you, urging you on. Then you can put aside everything in the present that might distract you or drag you down.

Some people hear this and they know, right away, what it means for them. Recently I was talking to a young, outgoing man named Sean who got his first job as a building porter. I asked him about his family and this was his answer: "Oh, you know. If they're happy, I'm happy." That's someone who already knows what gets him to work in the morning and what leaves him satisfied at the end of the day. Where he wants to be is wherever he can go to keep his family happy—and I have a strong feeling it won't be working as a building porter too much longer. So if your vision of where you want to be isn't yet clear, set aside a little time to study up on your most important client.

THE SOURCES OF VISION

WHERE CAN YOU LEARN to see where you most want to be? For me, I feel it most when I go back and revisit in my mind the places I don't ever want to be again. As I said, I've had many experiences I never want to repeat, and I don't want people I care about to live through anything like them. The memories of those experiences remind me of what I don't ever want to see again, and what I wish for instead—where I want to be. So ask yourself:

- Where have you been that you don't ever want to go again?
- What would your life be like, if it was safely past those times?

These are hard questions to ask, but they're powerful in the way they remind you that you know, deep down, what makes you tick. If you can recall the hardest times, you'll remember, deep inside, what you're working for.

If you are not the sort of person who can look back and bring up detailed memories of hard times, or if you can but you would rather not, then focus on the moments that energize and excite you. Try observing your thoughts for the next few days. When you have a free moment, sum up for yourself:

- What are you thinking about in your free time?
- What are the situations that interest you, fill your thoughts, or intensify your emotions?
- What calls you to action? When do you feel most competitive or most inspired?

Those feelings should offer clues to what you want to put behind you, and where you want to be.

Sometimes it is the more fortunate people who struggle to find their vision. I've wondered whether this would be a challenge for my own children. My wife, Jennifer, and I have worked as hard as we can to keep our kids from knowing the circumstances under which I grew up. If we succeed, our kids won't ever get that degree from the school of hard knocks. Already, when I talk to my oldest son, I realize that his childhood experiences are unlike mine in so many ways. He's having a real childhood, with little exposure to the frightening and inappropriate underside of the adult world. He has parents who have stayed together to do their best to make a loving home. He takes for granted so many things I didn't have, like good clothes and new toys and quality schools. He has parents who come to his school performances and his ball games. I used to wonder: will he be able to find his vision?

Then I saw that already he could tap into a vision of where he wants to be. I remember when he started playing in Little League. One day his team lost and when the game ended he cried in my arms. I told him it was all right, you played a good game; you'll get 'em next time. And he said no, I struck out twice. I could see in his eyes how much he wanted to win. He could see himself there already, in his mind's eye, getting those hits. That was his current vision of where he wanted to be—successful on the ball field. And so I could help him start to find the practical steps to get there. I told him, "You want to strike out less, get more hits? Let's take some time for extra batting practice. We can start today." I'm not suggesting he's going to become a professional ballplayer. He is still a child: it is too early for career goals. But already he has a vision of himself becoming a better player, a winner, and that vision gives him the excitement to take practical steps toward it, which will make him feel better and move him in the right direction.

DON'T LOOK WHERE YOU DON'T WANT TO GO

WHAT'S SO POWERFUL ABOUT focusing on where you want to be is not just that it keeps you moving and inspired, but also that it streamlines your life and helps you to put aside and, frankly, to ignore so much that could distract you and bring you down. For me, as a teenager, when it got bad in our family, I asked myself: what can I do to make a difference? If this isn't the life I want, and if I can't change my parents (whose behavior I described in the introduction), then what can I do to get where I want to be?

I learned to give as little energy as possible to what might get me discouraged. When potential employers looked at me or my background and lost interest in hiring me, I might have felt bad, but feeling bad wasn't going to change them. I would try to focus on the things I could do that day, the objective progress I was making—the new shirt, the new pair of shoes—and put the people who didn't get me and the doubts out of my mind.

My mentor at my first law firm, Jack Swarbrick, liked to quote the head of a Fortune 100 company he knows, who says that the most important discipline for a CEO is not to get dragged into work that isn't the CEO's responsibility. "The most important thing I do," he says, "is to ignore ninety-seven of the hundred things demanding my attention." Jack's point is *not* that you should set three priorities and make sure you get them done. That's not it. He's saying that the most important thing is *to ignore the other ninety-seven*. The big challenge is to keep all that other noise and all those people asking for your attention out of your head. Because a CEO should address only the work it takes a CEO to address; anything the staff can handle, they should handle.

I've tried to be a wise CEO in everything I've done, starting long before I had done all that much. I always try to ask myself: what will make the difference here? What will get the record finished, the client satisfied, the race won? Can I ignore everything else? That intensity of focus is as important for organizations as it is for individuals, in every business and every industry, and it's as important when you're having success as it is when times get rough.

WHEN SUCCESS IS THE THREAT TO SUCCESS

PEOPLE TALK AS IF success and failure are opposites, and sure, I know what they mean. But the fact is, both bad *and* good times can block your next success if you can't see where you want to be. What typically happens when a company is enjoying success is that people stop looking at ways to keep improving. If they've got a big hit or a big star on their team, they rely on the magic of past success to draw business opportunities toward them and to keep their relationships going even if they're doing substandard work. In other words, they stop seeing where they want to be, stop working to get there, and instead they just see where they are now: look, we had a success! We've got a star! And so what success often means for an organization is that from then on, things get worse. Quality declines and money gets wasted because too many people feel they've already "made it" and they don't have to work at it anymore. Then one day, your customers or your sponsors or whoever your work depends on sees that gap between your reputation and what you actually deliver, and they don't want to tolerate it anymore. By then, success has blinded you to where you wanted to be, and you've lost your way.

I always tell the people who work for me the same thing I tell myself: don't get caught up in the hype. Maybe you're having a big year and you're meeting some big names. Maybe you just met Tiger Woods. Well then, go ask Tiger Woods what he wants when he picks up his golf clubs, and I bet you'll hear that what he wants is what he's always wanted—to play his best. To win the next tournament. He's Tiger Woods because he stays focused on where he wants to be.

HOW HARD TIMES ARE A THREAT

IT'S NOT AS IF tough times are guaranteed to make people see where they want to be, either. Living through a downswing in a business or in the economy overall, people tend to look everywhere but at themselves. Rather than fix what's broken and focus on where they want to go, they look outside. They place blame and wait for rescue. A once thriving business can start to feel like *The Wizard of Oz*. Everyone's looking for a brain and a heart and how to get back home; everyone's looking behind the curtain for some great wizard (in business we call them consultants), but the truth is that they themselves are the people responsible for their own past successes, and they may well have everything they need to be successful again.

The most important thing I want you to take from this chapter is that wherever you are, and whether you're coming off of a good stretch or a hard one, it's always a challenge to refocus on where you want to be. The year I became president of DEI, which I certainly consider a great year, personally, is a good example. I moved my family away from Indianapolis, where we had always lived, to Charlotte, and there was a lot to adjust to, a lot of strain. Everything was new for us except each other—I had a new job in a new field, with plenty of people in the press doubting my chances of success. We moved to a new house in a new city, near a new school for the kids. Jennifer left the city where she had spent most of her life and built her dental practice. It was a whole new life. When it went well it was incredibly exciting, but nothing goes well all the time, and there were more than a few moments when I wondered if it was all worth the effort and upheaval. I was feeling some doubts and some discouragement. What could I do for myself, my own "most important client"?

For me, at those moments, it helped to reconnect with where I wanted to be, and I did it in a very practical and personal way: by checking on how my kids were doing. Jennifer and I have worked for a long time to create an environment where the kids can be comfortable and confident, where they can learn to try their best and still feel the freedom to make mistakes. When I heard from the kids and Jennifer about their adjustment to their new school, and when I saw that the kids were getting good grades and good feedback from the teachers about their emotional strengths and their contributions to their classmates' experience, it made me feel we were having a success that mattered. I could see that Jennifer and I were having some success, doing for our kids what hadn't been done for me, and that helped me keep moving forward.

Of course, someone else might not look to their kids as a measure of their success. It isn't important what makes me tick; the only thing that's important is what matters to you. But whatever it is, check in with it regularly. Remind yourself of your past successes. Take a moment to notice how far you've come. Most of all, make it practical. My method is not to "look on the bright side" or "hope for the best," but to focus on a vision of where I want to be that includes practical goals I can reach. When I was a cook at Long John Silver's, earning money so I could buy myself some clothes, my vision was of a better life, but it included the practical goal of becoming shift supervisor. On the job, I observed my manager and the crew chief. At home, I studied the training manual and practiced the drills. I took the test and earned the position, and then I was one practical step closer to a better life. When I got to law school, I treated it the same way. I had a vision of myself excelling, and so I studied the successful students around me, worked to understand the goals and personalities of the professors, and in every way I could, I tried to learn the skills involved in excelling both in law school and as a lawyer. I use the same approach today, as my vision of where I want to be continues to evolve. The power comes from having a vision that includes practical goals I can learn, systematically, how to reach. That's how I got from where I started out to where I wanted to be.

CHAPTER THREE

Appreciate Everyone

HOW DO YOU TELL the difference between a valuable connection (someone who will help you to greater success) and a waste of your time? Between a contact to cultivate and one you can safely ignore? The answer is: that's the wrong question. I've found that every personal connection is worthwhile in some way, every person a potential part of my success—if I can learn to see how. Every person represents a mutual benefit waiting to be discovered, so don't waste that chance. That's why I ask myself about everyone I deal with: how can we benefit each other?

In other words, to get my third rule, I take my second one, *see where you want to be,* and apply it to my relationships, old and new, shallow and deep. I ask myself: am I seeing where this person and I could go together, or only where we've been? Once I find a common goal, big or small, that goal becomes my new vision for the relationship. That's what I mean when I say: appreciate everyone.

It amazes me how often people don't recognize all they could accomplish just by making use of the opportunities they have right now with the people around them. I remember when I acquired a new company for Dale Earnhardt Inc. whose public relations department had three talented executives. Before their company joined mine, the three of them worked as rivals, competing against each other for opportunities and influence within their own organization. Each one tried to do everything solo and nobody did anything well.

They were frustrated with each other and with coming to work. It was a mess.

I felt they all could do great things if they would stop working against one another and begin to appreciate one another as allies. But when I took them aside, one on one, to suggest it, they were doubtful. Kevin had an unusual professional background, and Tara said she didn't see how he could be any help to her. Kevin didn't like Tara's style. And Blair told me he was good at his job already and didn't need two others around, interfering.

It was like a family that didn't get along. They assumed the others would always be there, and took each other for granted. All they shared was competition. They didn't see that they could help each other succeed.

What did I do? I made Kevin the head of corporate communications. Now every request we got for information about the company went directly to him. But our biggest need, as they all knew, was to have more consistency in our *internal* communications: among our staff, within the company as a whole, and with our sponsors. So I made Tara our specialist in internal communications. Meanwhile, I made Blair responsible for media requests specifically for the drivers, our talent, which is the smallest but probably the "sexiest" aspect of our communications work. Now instead of competing for the same turf, each had a particular focus that was of clear value. Even more important, this new structure gave them reason to look to each other for help. Kevin now had so much coming at him that he *wanted* to hand off some of the requests that came in, so he didn't get buried under them. Instead of fighting to protect his turf, he accepted help and felt grateful for it. Tara and Blair quickly came to appreciate how good it felt to have more control of a smaller area, rather than feeling helpless and stretched too thin. They also discovered the advantages of having each other as peers they could turn to for advice. Before, they had been three competing jacks-of-all-trades, masters of none. Now, all three were independent "experts" with reason to consult each other.

Two months later I met with them again, and though I spoke to them one-on-one they all told me the same thing: *it's fantastic working together.* They said things like: *Now I don't feel overloaded all the time. Now I'm learning so much from the experiences of the other two.* They became real colleagues, they had a lot of camaraderie, and they liked coming to work more. I had changed their job descriptions, but they had made the most important change, which was to stop seeing one another just as competition and to start appreciating the opportunities they could offer. They were the same three people doing the same basic jobs as before, but work for them had become a different, more productive, and far more enjoyable world.

DO I REALLY MEAN EVERYONE?

I NEVER ASK WHO is a valuable person and who isn't. I never segregate people into categories of "keep" and "toss." Instead, I look at each person and ask *how* we could be valuable to each other. I look for everyone's possible contribution, and that surprises people. Because, really—do I mean you have to appreciate *everyone*? Even those who might have let you down, betrayed your trust, or hurt you?

Yes, that's what I mean. I know this isn't always easy. We all have our resentments. I've felt them myself—even, if I'm going to be honest, with my own mother. It was after my father died, when my mother found Traci and me and showed us that he had been lying to us when he told us she was dead. She had a new husband and a home waiting for us. I remember how people acted like this family reunion was a miracle, but the teenager I was then didn't see any miracle. In fact, I felt no interest in seeing my mother at all. As far as I was concerned, she should have stayed in Indianapolis and left Traci and me in Las Vegas. All I felt was anger over what had gone on between her and my father.

With the memories I carried, I could have worked up enough

resentment about my childhood to poison a whole life. In fact, the only reason my sister and I got on the plane back to live with her in Indianapolis was that my stepmother said we had no choice.

Yet in time I came to see that while my mother behaved in ways she may have regretted in the pain of a broken marriage, and while she may have been an alcoholic prone to sometimes violent outbursts, she was also devoted to us. Slowly we restored that relationship, and the good that came was simply amazing. It started in small ways. Once, the bathroom doorknob broke and I fixed it. From then on she told me, again and again, that because I liked to find out how everything worked, I was meant to control and run things: her Max would become a businessman. And when indeed I tried to become a businessman, she was right there, wishing for my success at least as much as I did. She had an expression she used a lot, not just with me, as people who knew her remember to this day. She would say, "Take care of your business, boy. Take care of your business." And she backed that saying up with action. When Mickey Carter and I got out of law school and started our talent agency on a shoestring, she even worked for a while as our office manager. She spent so much time taking care of Mickey's baby girl that she became like a grandmother to her. So despite our rough history together, my mother became an essential part of my success.

Maybe I was able to grasp that chance with her because I had lost my father so young. It was terrible to lose him, but it did teach me something: appreciate people while they're still around. Because once they're gone, no matter what they might have done wrong, you feel their loss. That experience showed me early on that you don't throw people away. Not even the people who disappoint you. Not even the ones who've done you harm. Thanks to that lesson, I was able to help my mother reach her goal of healing her broken family while she helped me reach my goal of launching my career. To this day I keep a picture of her high up on the wall of my office, to watch over me and to remind me: appreciate everyone.

Easier said than done, you might be thinking. And I know, it's a lot easier to leave for work in the morning with the *intention* of appreciating people than it is to get through the day without feeling frustration, dislike, and a whole collection of impulses that aren't very . . . appreciative. Not at all. So I would like you to ask yourself two questions.

Does your work bring you in contact with people who get on your nerves?

Do people at work sometimes make you bothered and upset?

If your answer to either question was yes, then I say: good. What's so good about it? That upset you feel inside is like a warning light on the dashboard of your car. It's shining to tell you it's time to tune up that relationship before the whole thing breaks down.

A RELATIONSHIP TUNE-UP

HERE'S HOW I DO it. For each difficult relationship, I ask myself, what is our common goal? It may be small or big, but there has to be some good that this difficult person can do with me. The only trouble is, I can't always think of anything. Not right away. So before I give in and get annoyed and say things I might regret later, when the relationship is upside-down in a ditch, I have to find something better to do. I take a step back and ask myself some more basic questions:

- What is this person good at?
- Is there anything at all I admire about this person?
- Is there anything at all that this person can do that I would like to get done, too?

Even a tiny potential benefit can be a place to start. Say there's someone at work you barely know, but even so, when you're waiting for the elevator at the end of the day he talks your ear off. Say this person seems to think he was put on earth to tell everyone in the elevator some news he just heard on the radio or read on the Internet, and the truth is that after a long day you just dread seeing him waiting by the elevators. It's almost enough to make you take the stairs. Maybe you've tried ignoring him, but he won't stop his friendly chatter. He's like a one-man radio station. And you may know it shouldn't bother you so much, but it does. Well, all right then. Good. The warning light on the dashboard is now illuminated. Go to your questions. What does he know that you don't? Are you the kind of person who forgets to check the weather before you go outside? Maybe you've just found your own personal weather forecaster, if only you'll stop feeling annoyed long enough to ask him what they're predicting for the evening or the next few days. He might just remind you to go back for your umbrella one night and keep you from getting soaked. That's a small thing, I know, but it shows how you can take a relationship that feels like nothing but aggravation and begin to find a benefit that's mutual: he gets a more enthusiastic listener and you get to stay dry on your way home.

Of course, to get more significant benefits, you're going to have to find bigger talents and strengths to appreciate in the people around you. How do you recognize those strengths? It comes back to listening to understand, but now you're going to combine the two kinds of listening I described in chapters 1 and 2. So far, I've talked about listening for what moves others and listening for what moves you. Now you need to do both at once, so you can hear the areas of overlap: What could move you both? That's what you and the other person can do together. And if you accomplish something together, that will give you both something to appreciate in the relationship.

What makes this challenging is that often what you need from others is exactly what you can't do, or don't like to do, for yourself. That might be:

- Skills, interests, and commitments you lack
- Qualities or abilities that seem dull to you or beside the point

- Talents or gifts that you envy
- Differences in philosophy, values, and dreams

In other words, part of what you're listening for now is the chance that this other person, who may be annoyingly different from you in many ways, has the piece of the puzzle that you're missing *exactly because he or she is unlike you.* It's not just a matter of tolerating your differences so you can find some mutual benefit. Very often, *the benefit is in the differences.*

When someone makes me uncomfortable, I like to ask myself: might what bothers me about this person, if it was used a different way or in a different situation, turn out to be a skill? Are the ways that we are different, or that we see the world differently, actually ways that person could benefit my team, and vice versa? They say in love, opposites attract, but in business opposites too often keep away from each other—and miss the benefits they could create together.

Here's an example. After my law school roommate, Mickey Carter, and I first started our talent agency, the big question was whether we could make it pay. We had signed gospel singer John P. Kee and a few others, but could we make our agency a viable business? Or would we just go broke trying? Despite our early success, we were hitting some serious obstacles. First of all, the kind of clients we wanted to represent, athletes and artists, were expensive to sign up. We were based in Indiana, but our potential clients lived and played all over the country. To sign up college athletes we often had to fly to visit both the young players and their parents, making multiple trips so we could compete with other agents who wanted to sign them as well. It was time-consuming and expensive, and the income we saw came in fits and starts.

We needed a steadier source of income to cover our expenses, so we took on general litigation work, the kind of legal work we had done when we clerked for big law firms. But this created a second obstacle: the more time we spent on the general litigation work, the more reliably the bills got paid, but the less time we had left to pursue the sports and entertainment clients that would get us where we wanted to be. I found I was handling the small details of running the business, and there were days I felt like those details were an ocean that could drown me. Our short-run solution to our cash flow needs was putting our long-run vision in jeopardy.

We decided to hire some younger associates to help with general litigation work. Young attorneys were excited to work with us because of our clients—we had hot new recording artists and big-name athletes in and out of our offices all the time. But we also found that exactly because these young hires were motivated by our music and sports clients, they got distracted by them. Being near celebrity went to their heads. We would find that they were spending time with clients or angling to meet them instead of doing the work we needed them to do. Soon they were asking to be taken off the litigation work entirely and moved over to the talent-agent side. Now we had even more lawyers in our small firm who didn't want to do the short-term work that would pay the bills. Instead of a solution, we had the same problem, multiplied.

One day, as our small firm struggled along, I got a letter from a friend named Lisa McCallum. We had clerked at the same large firm a few years back and I appreciated her both as a friend and as an excellent lawyer. In her letter she sent me an article about a sports agent who had secured his next-door neighbor as a client, then helped that client become a number one draft pick, launching them both instantly into the stratosphere of professional sports. In the letter she sent along with the article, she wrote, "I'm going to be coming back to the Midwest."

Her letter reminded me of a few things. First, it showed me that, unlike the young attorneys we had hired, Lisa was someone I knew—someone I trusted and felt sure I could rely on. I had worked beside her and I felt sure of what I could expect from her. Second, her letter showed me that she still understood my vision: that story she clipped from the paper—in which a talent agent gained sudden success by making common cause with someone he knew personally—was like a sketch of my dreams. I started to wonder if we should ask Lisa to join us in the firm, instead of these young associates who weren't working out. Lisa, I knew, wouldn't drown in the details—she thrived on handling the practical.

At the same time, as I wondered if we should make Lisa an offer, I saw reasons to hesitate. Frankly, she could not have been less like me. She had no special passion for sports and entertainment law. She was not by any means an entrepreneur or a risk taker. To Lisa, my vision of a sports and entertainment practice looked more like some cockamamy scheme. For her, practicing law wasn't about having a vision or taking unnecessary risks, it was about getting the work done. To some degree, I knew, even my partner, Mickey, agreed with her. If she was around, I was likely to hear a lot of questions and doubt from both of them.

Beyond the differences in our philosophies and tolerances for risk, Lisa was also different in more obvious ways. She was a woman, of course, and also white and Catholic. She hadn't grown up in the streets—she was from the north side of Indianapolis, the well-off area, and as a kid she went to prep school. Our firm was known, at that point, as a "black" firm, with mainly black male attorneys and black male clients. There was no way Lisa would blend in.

But that didn't concern me. I knew Lisa from experience and I knew I could rely on her. She was smart, hardworking, and loyal. She didn't share my dreams because she wasn't a dreamer, not in business terms. She was an executor, the kind of person who got things done, and that was what we needed. And so, as I tried to listen to understand both what she had to offer and what Mickey and I needed, I realized that it was her different ideas of what being a lawyer was all about, her risk-averse nature, even her doubts about my entrepreneurial dreams that made her a good choice. Her differences from me were either not relevant or they were actually benefits, if I could get past my own worries about them.

And so, despite our many differences—or, I should say, because of them—I came to appreciate what Lisa could offer the firm, and how we could benefit each other. Instead of sending a note that said, "Welcome back to the Midwest, and good luck," I said, "How would you like to work with us?"

Once she joined our firm, Mickey and I could focus again on developing the talent side of the business. Slowly we made it profitable. Meanwhile, she was doing the litigation work to bring in steady income that kept the lights on. She took over a lot of the detail work that I hated. And as we had success bringing in more sports and entertainment business, she shifted so that half her time was spent working on contracts for the artists and athletes we signed to our agency. She had the skills to do it all, and I never had to worry about her saying, "I don't want to do litigation anymore, I want to be with the sexy clients."

Did she question some of my more ambitious schemes? All the time. I had the benefit of getting to test my plans against her doubts, and to learn from those challenging conversations. My schemes grew less "cockamamy" because I had her around to question them.

Did it matter that she was the only white woman in a "black" law firm? Lisa remembers it this way:

> The only time it came up was if there was a joke; they would call me "Pollyanna." I came from a different background, a more middle class background, so I didn't always get the street references our clients used or recognize some of the subtler forms of racism the black attorneys would encounter sometimes. They teased me a little for not seeing the rougher side of things. If some hardcore rap client came to our office and then requested to work with me and asked for my contact information, they might say, "Sure, of course he wants the white Pollyanna."

> But in terms of doing our work together, it was not an issue. Mickey was black, Max was biracial, I was white, but working

together it was just like with little kids. They don't know the dif-
ference; they just play together and everyone is treated the same.
What I felt from the two of them was that they respected me; we
all respected each other, and so it was a good fit.

The need to *appreciate everyone* holds in every business I've ever
encountered. For example, consider a story told by Jim Herbert, the
president of Neogen, a global health care company. In the 1990s, as
the company grew, Herbert had a new idea for expanding the company's reach while staying true to its core mission, which was protecting
the global food supply. He called a meeting and he made a proposal:
"I think we should look into rodenticide." There were two small
companies in Wisconsin that might have been a good complement
to Neogen's work, and Herbert thought Neogen should buy them.
But the reaction at the meeting was terrible. "What?" was the general
response. "You want us to get into the rat poison business?" These
were people who thought of themselves as working in the health care
industry. They didn't want to be associated with exterminators. That
wasn't who they were or what they did.

How did Herbert respond? He was the president and he knew what
he wanted, but nevertheless he welcomed these reactions. He encouraged his team to express the full range of their objections frankly.
Then he made his case to them, as if it was his obligation to win them
over. The company's core mission, he explained, was to make sure that
food and animals were safe. Up to that point, they had achieved that
mission with products that diagnosed safety risks and treated them.
But now he said: if we're in the cure business, shouldn't we also be
in the prevention business? Wouldn't our clients prefer not to have
a problem in the first place? Rodents transport bacteria and other
contaminants that harm animals and spoil food, so let's prevent rodents from causing problems in the first place. The mission is not to
sell diagnostic tools and cures; it's to keep our customers safe. That's
why they rely on us. Isn't prevention a part of safety? When his people

heard him out, they began to recognize the logic of his plan. Getting into the rat poison business stopped sounding unpleasant or crazy. This new approach stretched their images of themselves—and for that reason, it started to sound like a benefit.

What impressed me about this story was how Herbert's entire approach showed his appreciation for his colleagues. He showed appreciation for their passion for the company by welcoming their strong feelings, even when those feelings were hostile to his plans. He showed appreciation for their intelligence and their insight by making a case to them rather than giving them marching orders. By showing appreciation for everyone, even those who most objected to his initiative, he won greater agreement for his plan. The company bought the two makers of rodenticide and soon achieved an even more important position in their industry.

APPRECIATE THE SKILLS THAT DON'T FIT THE JOB DESCRIPTION

IT HAS BEEN A hallmark of the most successful companies in which I've worked that we made use of people's skills no matter who they were or what their job was. It didn't matter if you were an executive vice president or the guy who emptied the garbage cans, if you could do something the company needed, whether on the marketing side or working creatively with the artists, you would get a phone call.

At DEI, to give a more detailed example, I was advised to hire personal security because some of the fans felt so strongly about Junior's decision to leave the company that emotions could run very high. I hired a man we all called Sarge, a former marine who had run a homeland security fusion center with the Bureau of Alcohol, Tobacco, and Firearms. But as I got to know him, I realized he wasn't just an experienced police officer with a great understanding of event security. He was also a serious racing fan with a deep understanding of the sport. The same protective instincts that made him so good at his job turned out to have an application at the track as well. He became a "spotter" for one of our drivers, which meant that he would stand on a roof high above the track with the other spotters and watch the race through binoculars, keeping in radio contact with the driver at all times. Since the death of Dale Earnhardt Sr., drivers have worn protective gear that immobilizes them in their cars so their backs won't get broken in a crash. But this protective gear prevents them from looking over their own shoulders. The spotters tell the drivers what's coming up behind them and warn them about accidents or debris on the road they can't see up ahead—any potentially dangerous conditions for a car going two hundred miles an hour. It's a uniquely NASCAR form of "security." With Sarge in this dual role, we all won: Sarge got a bigger, more interesting job using a wider variety of his skills and giving him the chance to participate in a sport he loved; and we had the benefit not just of his many skills but of the companionship of this admirable man who developed them.

APPRECIATE EVERYONE, AND LET THEM KNOW

I SHOULD BE CLEAR, though, that appreciating what others have to offer you isn't enough to move people. Just because I can see that you could do a lot for me isn't, in itself, going to inspire you to do it. In fact, if all I can see is what you can do for me, you might start to wonder whether I'm looking for a partner or just someone to use. So if I want you to work with me, I've got to make sure I not only appreciate what you can do, but also *make you feel that appreciation*. Sometimes, as in the stories of Lisa and Sarge, I can show my appreciation of someone's talents and effort by offering them a new job, but it isn't very often that one has a new job to offer. So I'm always looking for other ways to show my appreciation. This isn't a burden for me; I like to do it. It feels good. But it's also essential to making any kind of alliance or partnership work.

Here is a list of the approaches that have worked for me. Some of these I'm sure you use yourself. Some you've heard before. But I suspect that you don't know them all, or go as far as you could with them to show your appreciation, and you may not realize just how much it can move people to help achieve your goals, or how dramatic the results can be. The biggest dividends come when you go beyond the ordinary and push yourself to appreciate everyone, every time, so they can feel what a difference they can make:

1. **Give credit wherever it's due.** If someone tells me that I'm doing a good job, I always try to put it in context. I'll say, "Look, that's nice of you to say, but you have to understand that I've got hundreds of people working all day to make me look good. I stand on their shoulders." I say the same thing when I speak to the press. I know that there's nothing I do that doesn't depend on the work of others, most of whom are never going to go on television or get interviewed for any publication. I look for every chance I can to acknowledge that.

2. **Make it personal.** Most of all, I try to express my appreciation with the personal touch. That may sound old-fashioned, but being old-fashioned about appreciation makes it more powerful. Because the more high-tech our lives become, the better it feels to receive a handwritten note, a personal phone call, or an actual pat on the back. I like to acknowledge people's professional accomplishments by writing my congratulations on a news clipping and mailing it the slow, old-fashioned way. I acknowledge birthdays, too; you would be amazed how touched people are by a paper card in an envelope. And if I know someone really wants something, even if it's very small, I'll try to get it for them. For example, a lawyer friend of mine, someone I used to work with, sent me a CD of music a while back. It

was written and performed by a contractor who was working on his house—a contractor who turned out to moonlight as a country-and-western singer. My friend was impressed with his homemade CD, but he didn't know anything about the music business. He did know me, though, so he sent it to me with a note saying that this contractor was a talented guy, a hard worker and a good man, and was there any way I could help him? Now, I was not then doing any business with this lawyer friend, and I wasn't personally interested in country-and-western music. Still, I knew someone in Nashville who might be interested, and so I sent the CD on to my contact there with a personal note saying I hoped he would give it a listen. And why not? I was happy to show my friend that I still appreciated him, and happy as well to do what I could to help this contractor, whoever he was, to find success. After all, I knew what it was like to work hard at a job that wasn't my passion in order to get a shot in the music business.

I should add that showing your appreciation in personal ways doesn't mean that you have to go all soft or sweet, if that's not your style. I think of my old wrestling coach, Ron Reichel, one of the most intense people I've ever dealt with, a former marine who didn't care if you felt like he was your friend or not. His mission was to use the athletic room and the classroom to make you a better person, and in his very detached, driven, marine kind of way, he could figure out how to motivate you, and never stopped trying to make you do your best. But as driven as he was, he also showed us his appreciation: he would invite the whole wrestling team over to his house for dinner, and he and his wife would stay up the night before, cooking healthy meals that would help us maintain our weight class for competition. That's how he let us know how he felt, how much he appreciated all we did for the team. He didn't go soft on us, but the feeling came through.

3. Don't leave people wondering where they stand. I've been around too many people who make me wonder, what kind of mood is he going to be in today? What's he really thinking about my ideas, my performance, or my future with him? It's stressful to worry that way. It saps your enthusiasm for the productive and enjoyable things in life. So whether we're talking about a work environment, a friendship, or my own family, I don't want people around me to wake up wondering whether or not there's a problem. If there is a problem, I'll say so straight out. And if I don't, you don't have to worry. I work to make that true for everyone I deal with. I want everyone around me thinking about something good we can do together, not trying to second-guess my mood.

4. Put the past aside and appreciate people for what they can do tomorrow. Here is where my approach of trying to appreciate everyone starts to get a little more challenging. I've already told the story of how, as a kid, some of my friends' parents would have me wait outside the door, because they didn't think I looked like the kind of child they wanted in their home. I said that some of those people like to tell stories now about how they "knew Max back in the day," and how they "always expected great things" of me, and so on. Some of them have wanted to get involved with events I have organized as part of my work in music and in sports. Those events have also drawn people I approached at turning points in my career, when I needed investors or support—people who turned me down when I really needed the help, but now show up wanting to be part of my success. How do I respond when they come around?

One advantage of living by simple rules is that there is no confusion: I appreciate everyone, and so I've done my best to appreciate these folks, too. I may not remember the past the way they do, but there are positive ways they can be part of what I'm trying to accomplish now. So I say yes, these folks knew me back when I was a kid. I say they were part of my story. I say I learned from them. In some cases, what I learned may have been that people chase success and they may not always take a risk on you when you need it most, but I don't talk about that. Instead I say, let's see what we can do together, going forward.

CAN YOU APPRECIATE PEOPLE WHO'VE DONE YOU WRONG?

I WOULD BE LYING, though, if I said that this practice is always easy. In the last chapter I told the story about the doctor my mother worked for when she was a nurse, the one who agreed to let me visit his office when I was a teenager, so I could get to know his profession and how I might break into it myself. I described how he took one look at me and set out to discourage my interest in medicine every way he could. That might have sounded like the end of my relationship with him, but life is long, and as it turned out there's a sequel to that story. Years later, a talented young woman applied to be an intern at my law firm, and when I met her I realized that this young lawyer was the daughter of that doctor who had sent me away. So the tables were turned. Now he was the parent seeking help for a child who wanted to break into a profession where African-Americans were scarce, and I was the successful black professional in town, the one being asked to be generous with my time and my insight, and even to let his daughter work in my office.

So what did I do? I gave her the internship. My wife, Jennifer, didn't get that right away. "You did *what?*" she asked me. "You hired her? Why?" Jennifer is a very loving woman, and one way she expresses her love is to be protective of me and all those she cares for. If she feels someone is trying to take advantage, or if she feels that someone has been hurtful or dishonest, she speaks her mind. She said, "I can't be-lieve you would do that man a favor! Why did you hire her?"

Jennifer was upset, and she had her reasons. As we talked and I listened to her some more, I realized that there were at least two good reasons she thought I was wrong, beyond just her caring impulse to defend against someone who had hurt me in the past. First, she didn't understand why, as a practical matter, I would make that choice to help a man who had slammed a door in my face. How would that do me any good? Second, even if it was useful, she couldn't imagine how I could do it, emotionally. How could I find it in myself to be forgiving and welcoming of this man's daughter, when just the story of his treat-ment of me as a kid made her so angry?

As a practical matter, I have found through my whole life that it's better to maintain a relationship, even one that has its problems, than to break it off. You can't get any mutual benefit out of a relationship you don't have. And so I strive to live by the advice I've probably given to everyone who is close to me, whether in business or in my personal life:

- Don't burn any bridges.
- Don't hold any grudges.
- Don't wait around for apologies.

To me, it's practical. If you are waiting on the other person to make amends, you could wait your whole life. If you forgive them in your heart, you can be free today. So if you're serious about getting where you want to be and not just staying where you are, then you will find out pretty fast that you can't know what's around the next corner. You don't know in what direction God is taking your life, and you don't know what He has in mind for the person who hurt you yes-terday. Maybe the two of you will meet again and you will need each other. Maybe the situation you're so upset about now was the result of passing circumstances, and when circumstances change you will find you can get along, work together, and make something good happen. So if someone does you wrong, or if you leave a work situation with resentment and visions of revenge, I always say: put it behind you and look for what you can appreciate about that person or situation in the future.

This is not a new idea. In fact, its effectiveness has been tested pretty thoroughly over the years. In the Sermon on the Mount, talking about the wish for revenge, Jesus said, "Do not resist an evil person. If someone strikes you on the right cheek, turn to him the other also." But does turning the other cheek mean that you ought to go so far as to *help* that person? Jesus was pretty clear on that, too: "If someone forces you to go one mile, go with him two miles. Give to the one who asks you, and do not turn away from the one who wants to borrow from you."

In my experience, these aren't just admirable sentiments. They succeed. Given the choice between this beautiful spiritual teaching and sound business practice, I've found there is no choice. They're one and the same. Because while forgiving and moving on may feel hard, staying angry is even harder. Practically speaking, it's exhausting— holding a grudge and maintaining your frosty silence will wear you out. You have to let these things go or they'll drain away the energy you need to reach your goals. Have you ever seen a movie or a play about revenge? Have you noticed how they're always the same? The hero spends a whole lot of time and energy plotting and struggling and fighting, and in the end there's a big mess everywhere and a lot of people wind up dead. That may feel good to watch for a couple of hours when you need to let off steam, but when it's your own life or your own company that gets messed up, and your prospects and potential connections that get killed, it doesn't feel good for long. Who has the energy for that? To me, the best revenge is making more of yourself than someone else thought you could.

So my answer to Jennifer's first question—when she couldn't understand why I would give that doctor's daughter an internship—was that as a practical matter, putting the past aside was the most productive choice. But that didn't make it easy, and one thing I don't ever want to do is to give out advice that sounds easy but turns out to be only so much rhetoric. In the church community sometimes you hear quick answers like that, answers which make hard choices sound like nothing. People say, "You just have to let it go." They say, "Let go and let God." There's nothing wrong with those sentiments, nothing at all, but how are you supposed to do it? For me what matters is not just to give a surface answer that sounds good, but to dig down to the deep motivation that helps people live the most productive choices they can. That was what Jennifer meant by her second question for me: even if you think forgiveness is good business and the right thing to do, how do you find it in yourself to do it, especially if you start to get upset?

I feel a special obligation to teach what I know about this, because it has benefited me so much. Again and again, when I talk to the people who have influenced my life, people I trust for guidance, they point to what I call forgiveness as the practical key to my success. My brother says that what stands out to him about my life is that, even with all we went through, I didn't get hung up on the past—and that now, it's as if the hard times we knew didn't matter. In the same way, my former wrestling coach has said that lots of families at our high school had troubles like mine, including divorce, substance abuse, and early death. Really, what I went through was nothing special. He says that what might be special is facing up to it and not letting it hold me back.

Do I find it hard to forgive sometimes? Sure. I feel the same feelings as anyone else. If someone has really hurt me, I can get overwhelmed and lose sight of what I could otherwise appreciate in them, and what we might accomplish together. But I try never to let my feelings, whatever they may be, dictate my behavior. I try to remind myself that feelings will change, but what I say or do will last. To keep that focus, I ask myself, often: *what result do I want?* Then I try to break what I'm feeling down into small pieces. It's the same approach I take coming to work when I feel swamped by things that need my attention; I know that I have to prioritize, so I can knock them off one at a time.

Here are four ways in which I try to break down my feelings into more manageable pieces and find the understanding and forgiveness to see where I want to be and not where I've been hurt in the past. I don't always manage to use all four in every challenging situation, but they have all helped me.

1. **Include the one who hurt you in your goals—and feel your emotions change.** I have lived in places that were steeped in resentment and the wish for revenge. When my mother brought Traci and me home to Indianapolis after my father died, we found that all around the house she had family pictures in frames, but there were round holes in a lot of the photos. She had cut my father's head out of every shot. I can't say I didn't know why, and I myself still feel that same impulse sometimes when it comes to my stepmother, who was definitely the hardest person in my life to appreciate. Just recently someone showed me an old picture of her dancing with my father at a wedding. I looked at the two of them arm in arm in that old picture and I thought: *Get me some scissors. I'm going to cut him free of her.*

   Feelings like that always have reasons behind them. My stepmother was the one who took charge of Traci and me when my father was on the road. She was often drunk, high, absent, or all three. I can still see her now, barging back into the house at all hours of the night, screaming about something that made no sense to anyone. She made sure we knew there was no love between us. Sometimes, when she and my father would get into a fight, my Aunt Linda would take Traci and me out of the house. My stepmother's son would see us heading out the door and he would say, "If you're leaving, I'm going with you!" She seemed to offer nothing to any of us but hurt and disappointment. It's been only too easy to fall into resentment. Resentment of the way she fooled people, of how she kept up appearances. Even my aunt, who lived with us for a year, didn't know that my stepmother hit my sister or that it was up to me to make her stop. My aunt believes to this day that my father didn't know a lot of what went on in that house, which shows you that my stepmother didn't just fool visitors; she even fooled people who lived with her.

Even after my father died and Traci and I went back to our mother's house, my stepmother was still doing harm. There is a Jewish tradition that a year after a death, the mourning period ends and you return to the cemetery to put a headstone on the grave. When my Aunt Linda, who is Jewish, went to visit my father's grave after the year of mourning had passed, she learned that my stepmother had never even paid my father's funeral expenses.

Now my stepmother has passed on, but I still carry her memory. Can I put aside my resentments and appreciate her? I have tried to find a basis for understanding, forgiveness, and learning. I've tried because that's been the only way for me to survive: to pick up on the positive. I've followed the method I would use with anyone else, asking myself:

- What was she good at?
- Was there anything at all I admired about her?
- Was there anything at all she did that I would like to get done, too?

In time I realized that while I hated the way she used it, my stepmother's ability to keep up appearances was a powerful skill—to behave with the right etiquette and to present herself to strangers and even members of our extended family as stable and trustworthy. I saw how far it got her, and I learned that it pays to keep up appearances. Now, when I think of her, I try to let go of the anger and remember that she was, in this narrow way at least, educational. Focusing on appreciating even one small thing about her keeps me from wasting my time on the negative. And if I can appreciate her, then by comparison appreciating even the most challenging person I work with is a whole lot easier.

2. **See the story from the other person's point of view, and discover sympathy.** My stepmother had her own past and her own demons. There were reasons why she turned to alcohol, drugs, and violence. But the truth is, when it comes to my stepmother, I've never gotten very far with imagining it from her side. I was too young when I had to live with her to understand the history behind her awful behavior, and since she's been gone there hasn't been much opportunity to learn her story.

I've had more success trying to imagine the other person's point of view when it came to forgiving my father and coming to appreciate what was best in him. Of course, I will never feel it was right for him to steal Traci and me away from our family and tell us the lie that my mother was dead. But over time, and with the benefit of my Aunt Linda and others in his family to help me fill in the story, I found that we had a surprising amount in common.

My father's mother died when he was still a baby. His father remarried and his stepmother raised him until he was ten. The couple had two more children, my aunts, and then his father divorced his stepmother and left her with the children. So like me, my father lost his mother and then his father. He couldn't tolerate living with his stepmother, and she had never adopted him legally, so with her husband gone there was nothing she could do to prevent him from leaving. He made his own decision about how to live: he went to stay with his aunt across town.

In all those ways, I see now, I have a lot in common with the boy my father was. He lost his family early, and while I don't agree with his actions, I can understand now that when he took my sister and me away from our mother he must have felt he was trying not to lose a second family. Some years ago, I found a picture of him as a little schoolboy in a uniform. I had it enlarged and mounted and placed it on my office bookshelf. That way I can have my father as a boy near me. There aren't a lot of people who have been through the kinds of things the two of us have been through, and it's healing for me to remember that. I appreciate him as a fellow traveler.

3. Do something different than what was done to you. Revenge is sweet. At least, it is for a little while, until the consequences of the new harm you've just done come down on your head. Still, I know revenge has its appeal, and part of that appeal is the chance to *do something,* to take your hurt and your anger and turn them into action. So if you've been hurt and provoked and you're looking for an alternative to revenge, it helps to find something else to do, some action other than revenge that is true to your deep motivation and that helps get you where you want to be.

When I first went to New York, I was a consultant, but my goal was to start a gospel division for an existing record company. I wrote up a business plan with all my best ideas, and foolishly I let it get into the hands of someone who saw himself in competition with me. He took my plan and tried to implement it at his company without me, even using my own contacts. I was still a consultant to the company, but to keep me out of the way he put my office down in the basement. This went on for a year, by which point this guy's attempts to use my stolen ideas had failed. He got fired, and afterward, going through his office, someone found a sticky note that said, "Keep Max away from all my contacts." It was in this guy's own handwriting.

Now, from time to time, I hear that he talks about me. He says, "That Max is a great guy! He's a great friend! We worked together way back when." And I've never called him out. My wife has said she would have liked to keep that note in her wallet, waiting for an opportunity to whip it out and say, "Oh, yeah? What is this? I found it in your own handwriting, you liar!"

When she's asked me why I don't take my revenge on him, which a lot of people would say he deserves, I've told her this: That person has to wake up every morning for the rest of his life, look in the mirror, and see himself. I am grateful that I only had to encounter him once. I'm free of him now, and the reason I'm free is that I'm different. I honor that difference by not taking revenge. It helps me to keep to my rule and appreciate everyone. I appreciate people who may have betrayed me for helping me to discover how different I am from them. And I appreciate myself for being different.

4. **Know that the hard times are preparation for better days.** When it is difficult to appreciate others, I turn to my faith—not because my faith is always steady or clear, but because it isn't. To me, what spiritual conviction means is being committed to *having* a relationship with God. I may not always really understand that relationship. I may not always even agree with it. But I work to have the relationship, anyway, and look for the good in it. I look for the good when I can see it clearly, and I keep looking even when I can't. That practice has been a source of strength for me in everything else I do.

One teaching that has guided me is that God moves in mysterious ways. We don't always know the Lord's plan; we just know that there is one. So when I get frustrated, I try to remind myself that whether I can see it today or not, every challenge is preparing me for something greater that I'm supposed to accomplish down the road. Sometimes I'll go to a funeral and see a family so blessed that they had years where four or five generations were alive at once. There may be children who remember whole conversations with their great grandparents. And I'll look at that family that's so blessed and see that they bicker about some of the silliest stuff, driving wedges in between one another. If they had all the years together and didn't appreciate all that they had, and I had less but I learn to love the people in my life where they are and while I still can, who is to say that I'm the unfortunate one? My hardships gave me the opportunity to make the most of what I have.

DON'T PEOPLE TAKE ADVANTAGE OF YOU?

I'M SERIOUS ABOUT WORKING to appreciate everyone, about practicing patience and generosity and forgiveness in my dealings, both in business and personally, but sometimes when people understand this rule, they get worried. Isn't it risky to be so appreciative? Don't others take advantage of you?

I tell them, yes. There are some coldly calculating people out there who care for nothing except their own gain no matter how you handle them. But while some are like that, most are not. Among selfish people, most are capable of thinking beyond themselves if you give them a reason to do so. So sure, if you are willing to listen to understand then you're going to find that some people talk your ear off, telling you all kinds of things—whether business troubles or personal troubles—that you would never have had to endure otherwise. You may also find you get asked a lot of favors. (I remember at a certain point in my career, it began to affect Jennifer as well. She was the wife of the head of the company, and people were treating her differently.

One day she told me, "People come up to me now and they say, 'So . . . what does your husband do?' And when they ask in that certain way I just feel like saying, 'You already know what he does. What do you want?'")

I told her, I know it's a burden to be approached in this way, but hasn't it been a blessing for us, too? We have found so many great opportunities, so much good fortune and such a good life because we actually listen to people, and some of them have responded by taking us places that most people never get to go.

People always come to you with their agendas—but sometimes their agendas overlap with yours. I know that when I share information and ideas, when I invest in a new start-up, even when I take the time to try to mentor someone, I am not just being generous. As my own mentor, Jack Swarbrick, would say, I'm investing emotional capital. I remember the people who invested in me early on, the teachers and mentors who went out of their way for me, and I've come back to them with further benefits and opportunities.

But what about the ones whose sole agenda is their own, the true opportunists who only take and give you nothing? There are such people, as I've said, and for that reason I have to draw a line. I'm free with my personal time, with my ideas, and with sharing information, but when it comes to professional time, there are only so many hours in the day. If someone wants to use my resources or my name, which I've worked so long to build, arranging meetings and signing deals they couldn't have gotten without me, then in exchange for my time and the use of my brand we need to discuss how their endeavors are going to benefit my endeavors, which I undertake to benefit my family.

In other words, the way to keep from being taken advantage of when you are out there trying to appreciate everyone is to keep your own agenda in mind. Make sure that what you are appreciating in them is the possibility of benefit that is truly mutual. Appreciation does not mean being nice. It is the basis of accountability. When I show someone I appreciate them, that I recognize the good and the value they bring and I want to deal fairly with them, I am letting them know that I expect the same. It's like a contract: I will treat you with the respect you've earned, and I expect you to do the same for me. There are psychological studies that show that when you remind people that their actions have consequences for other people, they start to behave more ethically. That's part of the reason why institutions like schools and the army have honor codes: when you remind people of the standards they've agreed to, they are better at living up to them. But I don't need psychological studies to convince me of this, because I've seen it all my life.

That's the serious, ethical side of this rule. The other side is that it feels good and it can be a whole lot of fun. It's a spiritual and practical core of my life, but it is also my idea of a great party. When I first moved to Charlotte, I threw a party that wasn't like the usual gatherings in any industry, where it's all the usual people schmoozing in the usual cliques. To start with, at my party, hardly anyone knew each other. There were influential people from the music business, major league baseball, and NASCAR of course, mixing with noninfluential people, neighbors, and friends. What all these different people had in common was enthusiasm to figure out what they could do together. People got to talking and they realized, hey, not only do we have a lot in common, but we have plans we want to develop and businesses we want to grow. I think everyone walked away that night with some new connections, but also with some specific plans to get moving on. It was a whole house full of people looking for ways to appreciate one another, and it was the dopest party I've ever thrown.

CHAPTER FOUR

Show What's in It for Them

ONCE, DALE EARNHARDT INC. was having a hard time with the press. The only pieces they were writing about us were gossip pieces that made us look bad. I felt like I was on the phone all day talking about irrelevant personal nonsense that was never going to help us move forward. I needed some way to get the press interested in writing positive, substantial pieces about the progress our company was making and all the good work our people did, but how could I influence the press? I had no special leverage, no magic. They were free to write whatever they chose and they didn't have to answer to me.

I did know, though, that even top reporters were working people like me, with the same deep motivations: doing their jobs to feed their families and reach their dreams. So I made a list of the journalists I most wished would write something positive on us, and I called them up. I had personal conversations with each of them, and I asked them how their work was going and what was on their minds. Then I said: "Listen. If you want to go on scooping gossip, don't bother calling me anymore. But if you want to break accurate news about our company, I will get it to a choice few of you as fast as humanly possible."

Of course, I had an agenda, but pushing my own agenda wasn't all I was doing; I was also showing what was in it for them. I could get them the scoops that would make their jobs easier and at the same time make them more successful. That got their attention. They started writing more substantive pieces, I stopped fielding so many calls about rumors and innuendo, and we were all better off.

The fact is, everyone is on the take. Everyone is always wondering: What about me? What can I get? That may sound harsh at first, but what it means is that other people are looking for personal benefit and gratification, just as you are. Just as I am. So although the recipe for success is a little different for each of us, the main ingredient never changes. That ingredient is *benefit*. If we're going to work together, we have to do each other some good; otherwise, what's the point? In chapter 3, I talked about the importance of appreciating others; now you need to make sure they appreciate you. To do that, you have to show what's in it for them.

This rule has been the source of some of the most important opportunities in my life—even, to be honest, before I understood it. When I was still in high school, trying to do my best in academics, in sports, and as a member of the community, I didn't understand that schools are like people and companies—they have self-interest, and they tend to reward the people who can help them meet their own needs and goals. I had no plan to do that when I applied to colleges, no understanding of how those things worked at that time, but our school principal, Don King, took the initiative. He had read an article by Monk Malloy, president of the University of Notre Dame. President Malloy had been a basketball player before he entered the priesthood and eventually rose to the head of the school administration, and his article said that Indiana colleges were not doing a good job of admitting Indiana students. Principal King read that article and remembered that he had once met President Malloy, so he called him up and said something like, "We met a couple of years back, and I understand that you need some good black kids. Here's Max Siegel: he's got great grades, he's a fine athlete, and he's president of his class. Will you take a look?"

I believe that phone call made the difference in my acceptance to Notre Dame, which in time led me to law school and everything that followed. Only later did I understand that my principal's call succeeded because he was showing the university president what was in it for him and for the school as a whole: a chance to live up to their stated goals of accepting more applicants from within the state. We weren't asking for a favor, we were helping them satisfy a need. And we kept doing it—over time, the principal recommended a few more students, and I would put up promising minority students in my room when they visited, to help them see why they might want to attend what was then a mostly white, mostly Catholic school.

THE CYCLE OF SUCCESS

OF COURSE, ONCE I got to college, all kinds of new opportunities opened up for me. It might seem obvious to say so now, but going to Notre Dame was an enormous change in my life, like moving up to the next league. It might never have happened to me, but once it did, I began to see that although success doesn't come according to our plans, it moves in a kind of cycle. You face a challenge, you meet it, you show someone what you're capable of and what's in it for them, and you may be blessed to find that the cycle begins again, at a higher level. Now you're on a bigger stage and there are greater rewards if you succeed, but the challenge is the same: *show what's in it for them.* I suppose I knew it worked that way in sports—how excelling in your local league could get you sent to regionals, and winning there could get you to nationals, and so forth—but now I saw that a similar cycle is at work everywhere.

Mickey Carter and I benefited from the cycle of success when our first talent-agency client, John P. Kee, became well known. As John traveled, and even in his concerts, he would publicly thank us for being his attorneys and ask his audience to pray for us. Others who wanted to become recording artists, or who were recording artists already but hadn't achieved the kind of success John was having, started to think about their lawyers. Many of them didn't even have lawyers, but now it occurred to them that a great representative might be what they needed to move forward. So they began to seek us out. When they considered hiring us, they could see what was in it for them because we had gotten results for John and he was happy enough with us to say so. Our client list grew and our success expanded across the gospel music industry.

It reminds me of the parable of the talents, in which Jesus describes the kingdom of heaven as a man traveling to a far country. The man leaves his servants his money based on the abilities he sees in each one. One of his servants is given five talents of gold, which he uses to earn five more, and when the man returns and sees the result he says, "Well done, thou good and faithful servant: thou hast been faithful over a few things, I will make thee ruler over many things." That to me describes the cycle of success: right now, whatever funds or opportunity you have been given, you have a chance to use them wisely and increase them. If you do that, then like the good and faithful servant you will help to create another chance, this time with greater funds and greater opportunities. It's not a "master plan." You have to take each cycle one at a time. But it can lead to results that no master plan can achieve.

One day, the great baseball player Tony Gwynn, arguably the best hitter of our lifetime, found my name on the back of one of John P. Kee's albums. He and his wife, Alicia, were interested in having John perform for some underprivileged kids in Southern California, where they lived. I was happy to help them arrange that concert, but my interest in them didn't stop there. As I got to know them, and we began to develop a personal relationship, I learned that they had been robbed blind by Tony's agent, who had robbed others as well. Forced to declare bankruptcy, they were now rebuilding. Tony was still young and already a star, so many agents would have liked to sign him up, but he was extremely hesitant to trust.

I knew there was an opportunity there, but I knew that any further success I could have with Tony and Alicia was going to come from showing what was in it for them, and that high on their list was going to be trust. As we got to know each other, Alicia began to ask me to handle a few small legal matters for them—responding to business proposals he was pitched, small disputes, and concerns having to do with the church. These were not the services that most people would have offered to provide for Tony Gwynn. Sometimes it was making payments on his existing deals or even picking up his car. Too often people look for the most glamorous or most obvious opportunity, but my attitude was that nothing he asked was too small or too big; nothing was beyond me or beneath me.

When did I pitch him on giving me a bigger role? I never did. I just made sure I was there to handle whatever came up. I was faithful to the small things without looking for the big payoff. Whatever they asked me to do, I made sure I got it done in a way that made them think, wow, look how much Max does for us. Look how beneficial it is to have him as part of what we do.

When our personal relationship was solid and the time was right, they asked me to become the Gwynns' general counsel. Of course, for Mickey and me that was another huge step. Everyone in baseball respected Tony Gwynn, and along with his endorsement came new credibility and the chance to meet with and sign other players, to meet with the general managers and owners of teams and with the Major League Baseball organization. Once again, the cycle of success brought us to a higher level, because we had listened to understand Tony and Alicia's needs and then presented our services in terms of what was in it for them.

DON'T SELL TOO SOON

HOW DO YOU SHOW others what's in it for them? I want to start by describing the one basic mistake that prevents so many talented, promising people from turning one success into an ongoing cycle. That mistake is to start pitching oneself too soon. Even those who understand this as an abstract idea may find that when they sense an opportunity, all they do is toot their own horn: "Look what I've done! Look what I can do! Look at my great resume, my expensive suit, my big new ideas!" It happens to me all the time. People start pitching me on the services they want to offer my company, or the things they want to sell me personally. But while they're talking, I'm thinking: Wait a minute, you may know my title but you have no idea who you're talking to. I don't really care how great you and the whatever-it-is you're selling may be, because I don't use those in my company. Or I have someone in the company already who handles that. Or you're talking to the wrong guy altogether.

FOCUS ON YOUR CLIENT, NOT YOUR SALES PITCH

HOW DO YOU AVOID selling too soon? To begin, take the focus off yourself. Just like in a first meeting, when it's important to put your own agenda on hold and take time to make the other person comfortable, so too if you want a long-term business relationship you need to set aside your agenda and focus on what the other person needs. When people go in selling first, they're forgetting that in the art of the sale, the salesperson has no say. It's the other person who is going to say yes or no, the other person who is going to commit—or walk away. Nothing matters unless that other person is moved.

I started my professional life as an attorney, and attorneys are not trained to be salespeople. Even so, we still have to sell our services to land clients. If we're trial lawyers, we also have to sell the jury on our interpretation of a case. If we're representing talent, we have to sell our clients within the industry to get them the most favorable deal out there. So in all those ways, lawyers, who are supposedly not in sales, still have to sell. And in fact, everyone's work has an element of sales, even if your work today is to get the kids to settle down and get dressed so you can all get to the zoo.

As a lawyer, I learned that I had to be absolutely devoted to my clients. I made myself available at all hours of the day and night, and I was willing to do whatever I could to take care of them and ensure the success of whatever project we were working on. That devotion helped me to keep clients and to succeed as a lawyer. Then in time I realized that it isn't just in the law that this is true. Whoever succeeds or fails based on your job performance is a "client." Whoever depends on you to come through for them is a "client." No matter what business you are in, you have clients, whether you call them by that name or something else.

The secret to success with clients, no matter what business you're in, or even if you're not in a formal business, is that they don't need you all the time—in fact, most of the time they don't need you at all. But when they really need you, you must have time for them. Day or night, when that call comes you have to go the extra mile and then some, and then some more. They have to see that you're not counting miles; you're committed to staying until you get results. Because while clients may be adults with power and responsibility, when it comes to their lawyers they want to feel the way children want to feel about their parents—they want to feel, "he was always there for me." Some clients may not need you for years, but then suddenly there is a crisis and if you're there, they will be grateful and happy for the years they paid you and didn't need to call you. But if you're not there when they need you, it's as if you were never there, or you never had the right skills.

EARN THEIR TRUST AND DISCOVER THEIR NEEDS

ONCE YOU HAVE YOUR focus on your "clients," you need to discover what they need—not in a general sense, but specifically. Anyone can promise and generalize. Anyone can say, "Baby, I'm going to make you a star," or, "We offer an exceptional value proposition." What's rare is to be able to go beyond the smooth talk and the flash and show the other person that you have something specific that he or she needs. It may be a particular skill or understanding that others don't have; it may be a quality of your relationship, like the trustworthiness and loyalty I offered the Gwynns. It's up to you to figure out what that skill or quality is. To do that, you have to be able to answer these four questions:

1. **What are this person's objectives, and what is getting in their way?** What separates your client from each of his or her goals? Is there something specific you could do to help them overcome those obstacles? I like to write out my questions and my answers. The reporters I described at the start of this chapter all wanted to do a better job in less time. Fine, but how? I had to take some time and think about the steps between them and their objectives. What do reporters do? They report stories. Where do they get stories? They interview sources. Ah: one thing reporters always need is more access to better sources. It was up to me to realize that, from where they stood, I was a "source"—so the specific benefit I could offer them was better access to a NASCAR source: me. I could be a step on the path to reaching that objective. That was what was in it for them.

2. **What impact will my own plans and goals have on my client?** I didn't just want to do favors for reporters. I had a plan of my own. I wanted to reduce their reporting on gossip about people in my company. That plan of mine was going to make

it harder for them to do their jobs, because they would have to find other stories. So I went to them and I told them directly, I want these gossip stories to stop, but I can give you something else instead. In that way I anticipated the impact my plan would have on them, and made sure that even as I achieved my own goal, my plan helped them more than it hurt them.

For the most important relationships, I write out my questions beforehand, with specific notes on what I know so far about the answers, to keep me focused during conversation. Research and other people may be able to help you think about these questions, but in the end you have to find the answers yourself. As you're working it out, you can mix a direct approach with an indirect one.

3. **Will they respond to the direct approach?** Sometimes it works to go to people directly and ask them what they want. I said in chapter 1 that if you have already established a comfortable conversational relationship, in which the person is relaxed enough to share feelings, impressions, and hopes, you can go beyond the networking talk and start to ask more focused and specific questions about what the other person needs. In that first chapter, you were trying to discover their general motivations, the areas they cared about. Now, you need to discover the specific services you can provide. Sometimes, your discovery of their needs may happen over months or even years, as it did with Tony Gwynn. But the moment will come when you will feel comfortable to ask direct questions:

- So, what are you hoping for in all this?
- What's your next step?
- What's a home run for you?

Similarly, you might ask about what's blocking their way, what they find frustrating about their job, or what they wish they could hand off to someone else. As with all listening to understand, it's often best to leave questions open-ended. Allow room to talk about whatever they want to talk about, and remember that most people don't get an interested listener all that often. They may need a little while to get used to it, and then they may say things they didn't know they were going to say.

4. **Do they need an indirect approach?** I find that although talking directly about what you can do for someone else is often the quickest and—naturally—the most direct, it doesn't usually get you everywhere you need to go. That's because most people, most of the time, won't say exactly what they need. Sometimes that's because they're holding back, but more often it's because they can't see all of their options. There are many paths we all could take, and none of us can see them all. We need help sometimes getting clarity about our goals and being creative about how to reach them. And so, separate from the direct conversations I may have with people, I try to do some private thinking about their objectives. I ask myself questions on their behalf:

- If I were in their shoes, what would help me reach my objectives?
- What approaches have I taken in the past, or seen other people take, to solve problems like these?
- Could I suggest a similar approach?

Finally, I try to remind myself that we're all human, with human feelings and blind spots. That means that sometimes our feelings keep us from seeing—or daring to try—a perfectly good solution that's right there in front of us.

BECOME THE ONE WHO CAN PROVIDE

NO MATTER HOW MUCH you can learn about someone else's needs, or how inventive you can be about discovering how you might address them, in the end they are going to want more than your understanding and your creative questions. They'll want results—practical, high quality results they can measure. How do I know that? Because it's the same thing you would want if the situation was reversed. Imagine you hire someone to do a job for you. What do you want from them? It doesn't matter whether your goal is to launch an ad campaign, meet a production deadline, get a new product to market, or repair your car. You want them to do the job they were hired to do—and do it well. Other people are no different. They want the same from you. If you can deliver high quality results, they will be satisfied and they will be inclined to work with you again. But if you aren't up to doing your job, or if you don't come through for those who depend on you, you can believe they will notice.

Maybe that sounds like something you already know, but again, it's not an issue of knowing. You have to live it. I remember my mother, who never had a lot of patience for my father's talk about working hard and waiting patiently to get a little of the real thing. She had many good qualities, but she was not interested in waiting for appliances and electronics. So she shopped from the Fingerhut Catalog, a poor man's version of a credit card. I would come home for a visit from college and the house would be full of her new purchases—once it was a refrigerator, microwave, stereo, and television, all for $200. Meanwhile I had spent $600 on my television. She had a whole roomful of new stuff, and I had a bare dorm room with just a television. The first time I came home and saw her living room, I thought, wow, maybe she's onto something. I was always on the lookout for a good shortcut, and I thought that maybe there was a shortcut my father didn't understand.

Soon, though, my mother's new television broke down. She had to get another and another one after that. Often what she ordered broke down before she even got it paid off. Meanwhile, my television worked for years and years. So the lesson seemed clear: when it comes to getting quality, there are no shortcuts. But again, knowing the lesson is just a small part of it. The challenge is to live that lesson every day.

HAVE THE PATIENCE TO BUILD YOUR SKILLS

THE APPROACH IN THIS book only works if you can deliver results. Delivering results means putting in the time to build the skills you need, whether you're at the entry level, at the very top, or somewhere in between. You have to learn what it means to do your job well, and to understand who depends on you and how you can take care of them. Most of the failures I have seen have been made by people who got too far too fast, and didn't know how to handle themselves.

Every kind of job has its core competencies, those basic skills that, when seasoned by experience, bring success. There is no substitute for developing those competencies and getting experience using them together. I see it among my colleagues in architecture or design, who have to learn to take a practical skill set (drafting, sketching, computer-assisted design, and so on) and unite it with their unique sensibility for what will compel a consumer in their particular industry. I see it among managers, who have to build an understanding of the overall operations of their organization while at the same time learning to listen well enough to hire and direct people who know parts of the operation better than they do. I see it in marketers and publicists, who have to take the time to learn how their consumers' buying habits are evolving and the channels, old and new, by which they get their information. It's different for every kind of job or business, but what they all share is this inviolable rule: you have to put in the time.

What if you don't? Early in my career, there was a young guy at work who was always trying to one-up the rest of us, always politicking and trying to get an edge with senior management. Sure enough, by age thirty-five he had convinced enough people that he was some kind of genius. He was put in charge of a whole division. There he was, making all kinds of money, with an impressive title and a big, beautiful office. Meanwhile, I had been trying to learn my job as well as I could, so I could demonstrate some real results. After seeing him leap ahead of me, I have to admit that I questioned my approach. It had been pretty easy for me to watch my mother's parade of broken televisions and draw my conclusions, but it felt different when it was my own life. I didn't want to wait while someone else got all the perks. Why couldn't I coast along and rely on my friends in senior management to get me a corner office? People succeed that way all the time, don't they?

Yes—for a while. But I've learned that shortcut success doesn't last any better than cheap knockoff televisions. *You have to season your talents with appropriate experience.* Otherwise, even when you can see the finish line you'll find you can't cross it. My colleague who had politicked his way into a high-level position, who seemed like he was sitting on top of the world, was really in over his head. He looked great but he performed poorly. His division fell behind the others in the company. When he had to make tough decisions, he didn't have the experience to make the hard calls or to help his people through their doubt and stress. At thirty-five he was sitting on top of the world, but by thirty-seven he was just sitting around, trying to figure how to get back to being the next big thing. And he never has found his way back. He became known for his failures, and no one wanted to give him a big responsibility again. He had gotten his success without getting results, and it ruined his career.

My dad used to tell me, "A little of the real thing is better than five pounds of phony." To him, owning one good pair of shoes was better than filling your closet with cheap ones. He believed that quality and substance stand the test of time, whether in shoes or in people, and so it was worth the wait.

SHOW THAT YOU CAN SERVE ANOTHER'S VISION

IT'S NOT ENOUGH TO develop the skills; you also need to show your clients that you will use those skills in the service of their vision. When I was working for Tommy Boy Records, the head of the company, Tom Silverman, lost his second in command. Once she was gone, others in the company sensed his weakness and began trying to wrestle control away from him. I knew that not everyone in the company was loyal to Tom's goals, so as I worked on the tasks he gave me I also worked to show him that I could take his vision and make it operational. The music business can be a world of "me, me, me," but I tried to show Tom that not only did I have the necessary creative chops for the job and the organizational ability to hold others accountable for their deadlines, I was also on his side.

In time he put me in charge not just of his gospel division, an African-American music form, but also of Artists and Representation (A&R) for the entire company, making me responsible for finding and helping to develop all our talent, black and white alike. I can't express to you what a huge accomplishment that was; so often in the music business, black executives are limited to working with black artists. But while that was the specific issue in my career at that time, the fact is that whenever anyone receives a promotion or an expansion of responsibilities, it's because the person bestowing that opportunity can see beyond the present arrangement of the company and imagine what in the new arrangement after the promotion will be in it for him or her. Tom Silverman's choice to promote me took vision and guts, but it wasn't charity: I had shown him what was in it for Tommy Boy.

FIND THE HAMMER

SO YOU'VE GOT THE goods, you understand how they're valuable, and you've presented them sensitively, making clear what's in it for the other person. But you're still not getting the positive response you want. What's wrong? It may be that you're not talking to the right person—or rather, that someone in the background shares responsibility for your client's big decisions. Most people tend to lean on others for guidance. They ask, "Should I take this job? Should I invest in this company? Is this what's right for me?" The most influential advisor may not be visible right away—rather than a manager or parent or spouse, it might be a choir member, a grandmother, a distant friend. You may never know who else has to sign off on what you want to do unless you establish the trust that lets your potential clients share their concerns and show you who has the influence. Once again, you may not be able to learn everything you need to know directly; you may need to get to know your clients better, in some ways, than they know themselves.

Once you identify the key advisor, you may need to meet with that person yourself. As a talent agent, I found this all the time when I was hoping to sign up college athletes. My partner and I learned that we might have to make two trips, one to visit the athlete at school and another to meet the parents back at home, because no matter how the kid dominated when he was playing ball, he still went home at night to get advice. That's why our motto was: *find the hammer.* If you want to build something, it's not enough to have a pile of lumber and a box of nails. Nothing's going to get built until you find the hammer.

With Tony Gwynn, too, I would never have succeeded had I not recognized that he made his big decisions along with his wife, Alicia. She was the one who began offering me small jobs to complete for them, and as I did those tasks she was the one observing to see whether I was committed to her and to Tony as people or whether I was only looking for a big score. Had I not recognized that she was as important a decision maker as her husband, or had I tried to go around her to get to him, I might have missed the chance to know and to represent one of the most important figures and families in my life.

HELP THEM WITH THEIR BAGGAGE

SOMETIMES, EVEN AFTER YOU focus on the needs of the person or organization you want to work with, and even after you earn their trust and demonstrate that you have the skills they need—not just to them but to their most trusted advisors—you still can't close the deal. At that point, you might feel like you're hearing that old breakup line: "It isn't you, it's me." But just because you find that the person or organization you want to partner with has some personal issue or some old baggage that holds them back, that doesn't mean it's time to walk away. If their baggage is too heavy, offer to help carry it.

When it comes to sensitive issues that scare people away, it may be enough to acknowledge that some subjects are sensitive, then make it clear that you will leave those topics alone. I know that this approach works because it has worked on me. Back when I was in college, after my baseball career ended, there was a wealthy Mennonite family that provided jobs and housing for a lot of the Notre Dame athletes over the summer. The family loved sports and they were charitable people, but part of their motivation was to have an influence on our behavior and our development. In particular, they wanted to encourage us to go to church. Back then, though, I hadn't yet discovered how valuable that could be. And especially once I got to college and I was free to do as I pleased, I was definitely going to take issue with anyone who wanted to instruct me on how to live my life. But they never lectured us or tried to micromanage us with rules. The family seemed to understand the kind of personal baggage that young college athletes would carry, and how they weren't going to be receptive to someone acting like their parents. They didn't lecture or preach. They just made one simple request: we could come and go as we pleased, but would we please go to church on Sunday?

To me, the interesting thing was that they succeeded. They had an impact on me spiritually. Not because they tried to persuade, but because they let me observe for myself that they were very successful in business, while at the same time they seemed like compassionate human beings. I observed how they lived, and how the family was close; going to church was part of that life. Mennonites come from a Swiss-German tradition that preaches pacifism (in other words, not a group of people I had spent time with or even knew much about), but what I saw spoke to me. In fact, I think all of us who were their guests walked away from them and from Notre Dame changed, because we had an example of a family like that. And to the degree the message got through to us, I think it was because they understood what might provoke an unhelpful reaction in young men away from home for the first time, and they shaped delivery of their message to avoid provoking us with lectures. They inspired me to reconsider attending church because they helped me with my emotional baggage.

• •

Emotional Baggage

After you consider the other person's objectives and the impact what you want to do might have on them, take some time to consider what you know about them emotionally. Before an important conversation, or when I feel things are coming to a turning point with someone important to me, I ask myself:

1. What do I know about this person's moods?
2. What kind of baggage and fears does this person bring?
3. How have I had success responding to them?
4. How have I gotten into trouble?

For each conversation with an important connection, prepare a short list of reminders, mentally or in writing, of what
you know to try and what you know to avoid.

• •

I suppose that experience with the Mennonites was in the back of
my mind in the days after Junior decided he would leave DEI to drive
for another team. He was a very volatile person, very passionate, and
when he suffered over something people often responded by walking
on eggshells. It seemed to me, though, that this extra care only made
him feel worse.

In the days after he made his announcement of his plans, I ran into
him at the track during a rain delay. I could see he was feeling badly.
Some people, I suppose, would have assumed that once he made his
decision to leave my team, there was nothing more for either of us
in having a relationship. But I didn't see it that way. What I did see,
by this point, was that in order to keep that relationship going, there
would be times I would need to help him with his baggage.

"You seem like you're in a crappy mood," I told him.

He looked at me and didn't say anything.

"All right," I said. "When you're ready to talk, you'll talk."

I thought we were done, but he said, "Maybe you're the person
who could cure me."

And so as we waited out the rain, he began to tell me that he was
scared to death that he might have made a mistake in leaving the
team, and that everyone in the sport would be angry with him. I told
him, "Listen—now that you've made your decision, you need to look
forward. Don't second-guess yourself. Do what's in your heart. And if
there's anything I can do for you at DEI, let me know."

"Are you sincere?" he asked.

"Of course I am," I said. "Your success is as important to this company as its own success. You're still a part of this family."

Up to this point, I had never tried to have a social relationship with him or with Kelley, but now he said, "Maybe you could come over to my house. We're having some people over this weekend." By his "house" he meant Whiskey River, his 160-acre resort.

We began to talk regularly about his career. And as I'll describe in chapter 7, there were benefits for both of us and for our respective teams, benefits that would be essential to my work to help increase diversity in NASCAR, the focus of my work with the Drive for Diversity program. That possibility remained open because I could help him in this way.

SKILL AND DEDICATION ARE NOT ENOUGH

OF ALL THE RULES in this book, *show what's in it for them* may be the one that people most often mean to follow, but don't. Yet it's so important to focus on the needs of the people you want to do business with that I want to tell a story of failure—one even more startling to me because it befell one of the most promising and ultimately successful young professionals I ever had the chance to mentor. She had all the skill and dedication to her work that anyone could hope for, yet she needed something more before she could realize her amazing potential.

My friendship with Ann began when she came to my firm for a short internship, to see what we actually did in a law firm. She fit so well with what we were doing that we asked her back over the summers while she went to law school. Ann was outgoing, hardworking, very smart, and personable—I wasn't surprised when she graduated law school and was hired to work in-house for an extremely prestigious business. Her career seemed to be taking off, but then she ran into difficulty.

The woman Ann reported to had many more years of experience, but she wasn't outgoing like Ann. She was more introverted and she kept to herself. When Ann went to meetings or company gatherings, she talked with everyone she could, but her supervisor didn't see that as valuable to both of them. She saw it as a problem. The supervisor began leaving her out of meetings and not inviting her to events, even when they related directly to Ann's work. Ann felt stifled and uncomfortable, like she was being kept in a box.

When it came time for her performance review, Ann got wonderful evaluations, the kind of e-mails that you save, except from her supervisor, who was lukewarm. She made a number of criticisms Ann didn't hear from anyone else. Then came a restructuring of the division, and Ann discovered she had been bumped down a level. When she said she felt demoted, the supervisor told her, "Well, now you have something to work up to."

When Ann and I discussed the situation, she understood that her supervisor was afraid of being upstaged, but she insisted that wasn't her intent. She told me, "In my mind I felt I could never outshine her— she was so much more accomplished in the profession and she had so many more years of practice. If I did a good job, didn't I make her look good? Wasn't that a mutual benefit?"

I told Ann, it ought to be enough just to have the skills and to do a great job, but in the world of human emotions it's not always that simple. Your job is always more than the work that you produce, no matter how good it is. Take a step back and consider what makes this person tick—which in this case seemed to be fear. You may not be giving her reason to fear for her success or for her job, but if that's the baggage she carries, if that's what she's primed to hear, it doesn't matter if she's wrong. Perception becomes reality. She's going to feel afraid anyway and her fear will make her hold you back. She needs reassurance.

Ann was very young then, and she was naturally direct. She felt that if there was an issue that needed discussing, then you should come out and discuss it. She went to her boss and said, "Look, I really don't want your job. I don't know that I would even be interested in it. And anyway you have fifteen years on me. Do you feel like that? Do you feel that I want your job? Because I don't."

Ann hoped this would address the boss's fear, but instead it shut the boss down. She gave Ann a stunned look and then changed the subject. They never had the frank conversation Ann had hoped would clear the air. It may be that exactly what frightened Ann's boss about her was how bold, confident, and fluent she could be in a charged situation—qualities that the boss lacked. The fact that Ann could speak openly about the boss's fear of losing her job only seemed to make her boss more afraid, and she continued to find herself left out of important meetings.

What had gone wrong? Ann had the skills to do her job, and she even had insight into what made her boss tick. But she wasn't able to put those insights to use because she had never fully established trust or shown her boss that she could meet her emotional needs. What did I suggest? I told her I thought she had a good understanding of the fear that made her boss tick. But knowing what makes someone tick doesn't always mean that you can work with her. You can't own someone else's feelings. Maybe, I said, you've done the best you can with her and now you need to find a work-around.

I encouraged her to form a relationship with her boss's boss and with some other allies who might, in time, help to pull her out of this situation. Not to complain to them about her boss, but to establish her own relationships. Ann worked in a field where a lot of the business was social, and as she encountered them in open, social settings, she found chances to ask them about what they were trying to accomplish. She also volunteered to work on certain projects just so she could be around those important folks in the company. As they became comfortable with her and saw that she could serve their goals, they began to come to her directly. Although her boss was too afraid to see the benefit in expanding Ann's responsibilities, these others in the company were not.

When Ann's supervisor noticed the change, she couldn't do much, because now Ann had her own relationship with her supervisor's boss, the head of the organization, and if he said he wanted her on a certain project or present at a particular function, the supervisor could only say, OK. There was still tension in the relationship, and Ann left about a year later for another job, but the problem was contained for long enough that she could leave on her own terms, for something better.

Of course, a new job doesn't mean you escape your old challenges. At her next job, her boss was already a friend. This time they were closer in age and in experience, but that can also be dangerous; it's easy in a competitive setting to feel threatened by someone you see as similar to you. As Ann saw, this boss was like the previous one in that she was very smart and hardworking but, compared to Ann, an introvert. Ann wanted to make sure that this time she prevented an emotional problem from developing, rather than trying to deal with it afterward. So I asked her, what are you doing this time that's different?

Ann said she was making a point of deferring to her new boss, offering opinions when asked but making sure her boss felt that Ann was not in any way trying to take over, and that the boss was in charge—after all, that was her role. In this new job, things went much better. Ann's boss was comfortable in the relationship and pushed her to take on additional responsibilities in her company, some that went beyond Ann's legal training. But had Ann not been sensitive early on to addressing her new boss's needs and showing what the benefit could be in letting Ann soar, it could easily have gone wrong.

THE FASTEST CARS AT THE TRACK

FOR ME, ONE OF the proudest examples of putting these principles into practice came when we consolidated the three different racing shops at DEI into one. The physical campus had always been broken up into a number of different buildings, and each one of the race teams had a shop dedicated to that one team. That meant that even though we had multiple teams, we weren't getting any of the benefits of working together: we weren't sharing information, comparing practices to see which was best, or achieving economies of scale.

The planners and engineers told me it would be most productive if all of the functions were handled in one building. That way all the cars could come off the assembly line in one place, with all of our experts focused on building the best possible car, and then giving each one the small final tweaks it needed for each individual driver. But although the experts agreed it was best to build all the cars in one place as a matter of engineering efficiency, psychologically the different teams were used to thinking of each other as competition. They hid their breakthroughs from one another and behaved as if their goal was to beat the other DEI cars.

I started talking to everyone I could about shifting focus from the individual teams to the organization as a whole. Instead of trying to keep their new developments to themselves, I wanted everyone working on the cars to share their competitive edge so the whole organization could be stronger. It was just as exciting to compete as one big team against the other teams as it had been to compete internally, every shop for itself, but I had to make the case to them in a way that acknowledged their expertise and their accomplishments.

The result was that these once separate shops consolidated and started turning out some of the fastest cars in the sport. In the qualifying runs at race after race, DEI cars were up front—and not just one car, but three or four together. During this period we were weathering the reaction to Junior's decision to leave and then the downturn in the economy, and it was a huge accomplishment and a huge source of pride to be able to point to our cars as they won the qualifying runs and say: look what the people of this company can do.

• • • • • CHAPTER FIVE • • • • •

Use **Your** Outsider **Advantage**

WHEN I WAS FIRST hired as president of Verity Records, there was a major new talent I wanted to sign, a gospel singer with huge promise both musically and commercially. So for the first time, I asked my boss to write a check that was much bigger than he expected. He didn't want to do it. He had made a career out of not overpaying artists and he guarded his reputation for knowing the value of a dollar. As he peppered me with questions and doubts, I could feel that to him I was still an outsider to the music business—I had come up as a lawyer representing artists, not as an executive in record companies. Would he trust my judgment on this big negotiation?

I figured I had two things going for me in his eyes. One was that I had a track record of recognizing musical talent. I had signed some great musicians as an agent, and that gave me credibility as I argued for signing this artist to a record deal. The other was that I spoke the language my boss understood, the language of business. I showed him my analysis of the demographics of the Christian market, making clear how we were going to reach deep into that market to sell enough albums to recoup our investment in this new singer. I didn't try to talk to him about the good that gospel music could do because I knew that wasn't his concern. He wanted to sell records, so I worked to show him with facts and figures why we could do just that.

Finally, my boss agreed to write the check. We were going to sign this great, as-yet-unknown artist for a million dollars and everyone

in the company was feeling: Let's go! Let's get this popping! We contacted the artist and told him we could give him everything he wanted
to support his next album. Did we have a deal?

The artist said, "I'll let you know in a few days. I have to pray
on it."

My boss was furious. All the good feeling that we had in the room
went sour. As soon as he got me alone, he asked, "What the —— does
this guy mean? We got him his money. Now it's business!" I suppose
he felt the artist was disrespecting the very serious offer we had just
made. My boss wanted me to go straight back and deliver an ultimatum: sign our contract or stop wasting our time.

I admit I felt pressure to do it his way. I was new at Verity Records,
and as I've said, I had an unusual background compared to others in
record company management. I worried that this breakdown in the
negotiations would give my boss new doubts about whether I fit in.
Should I show him I could act like an insider and do it his way?

As I say, I understood where my boss was coming from, but the
trouble was that I knew the artist saw it differently. It wasn't a question of right and wrong; they were just very different men. The focus
of my boss's life was business and he had been very, very successful.
(Later he would go on to sell his company for three billion dollars.)
But the artist, who was African-American, hadn't had financial success. He was a Southern minister used to making ten thousand dollars
for an album. Now we had offered him a million. I didn't understand
every last difference in their backgrounds, but I knew the two men
saw the world differently, and that the only person in the middle of
this endangered negotiation was me. I could see my boss's point of
view, but could I see the artist's?

I wasn't all that churchy, but I had grown up close enough to the
spiritual community to know something about how its members
operate. Before a big decision, they seek personal confirmation from
God. If that was what the artist was doing, I didn't see how delivering
any ultimatum would move things forward—from what I had heard,

God was not known for keeping anyone else's schedule but His own. So instead of acting like a record company insider and delivering my boss's ultimatum, I decided to get back to basics: what made this artist tick?

I went to talk to him, but instead of demands, I brought questions. Was he unhappy with our offer? Did he feel we weren't meeting his needs? He said no, he thought it was a very generous offer—but exactly because the money was so good, he was worried it was influencing him too much. Was signing with a big commercial company going to be true to the integrity of his ministry? Was this business deal in harmony with the vision God had given him?

Listening, I began to recognize the problem. For my boss, the size of the check should have answered all the artist's questions. But for the artist, it raised new ones. A big check wasn't going to speed up his decision making; it was actually going to slow him down. He told me again that he needed some time to pray.

What could I say to that? I said, okay, fine, but could he get back to us in three days? Meanwhile, I had to explain to my boss and the whole company finance committee that we didn't have a deal after all, because this person was off somewhere praying. What did I do? I told them the truth, but I told it in the language I thought they could understand. "He's considering our offer," I said, "and I think everything's going to be cool. He just needs to examine all the ramifications of the deal."

I had a few nervous days of waiting, but in the end, maybe because we hadn't rushed him or lectured him about how great the money was and how that should have been all he needed, the artist felt comfortable enough with us to sign. And I realized that as much as anything in my resume, what I brought my company was my outsider advantage: my ability to listen to what people unlike me said, to draw on my own experiences and imagination to understand what made them tick, and to help interpret those people for each other so they could work together. It was as if my boss and the artist were two foreign countries, and I had gone back and forth between them like an ambassador, helping them agree to a peace treaty.

To work that way, I had to find a new model of success. The old model of success that I saw around me was based on fitting in. We were all expected to adapt ourselves to the insider culture if we wanted to make it into the "club." And if we had elements in our backgrounds that didn't fit, or personal shortcomings or setbacks in our past, we hid them. Fitting in was how you got the insider advantage. But all this striving to fit in can cost us something even more important to our success, what I think of as the *outsider* advantage. In fact, if I hadn't turned away from fitting in and embraced my outsider advantage, I would have blown that million-dollar deal, one of the biggest deals of my career.

In the global business environment, where technology has now made it possible to do business with almost anyone, anywhere, we're all outsiders to some of the people we meet, at least some of the time. Every company that's looking ahead wants employees who can help diverse groups to relate and connect across their differences.

What differences am I talking about? Some may be obvious, like the physical differences of race or sex, or the speech differences of people who come from different places. Others are more hidden, like differences of childhood wealth or poverty, your hometown, religion, political party, cultural heritage, hobbies—even where you went to school or your previous line of work. In the new model of success, you don't bury all that, you bring it to the table. That's the outsider advantage—realizing that instead of working to hide or change what sets you apart, you can use it to understand and connect with coworkers, clients, or customers—and motivate them to work with you.

WHAT'S SO GOOD ABOUT BEING AN OUTSIDER?

I WANT TO MAKE sure that this valuable truth doesn't get lost, because it isn't necessarily what people are expecting to hear. I know that some might read that story of working as an ambassador between my boss and our promising gospel artist and think: Well, sure, this all sounds very nice for you Max, seeing as you're biracial and you grew up with gospel music and secular music. You had a foot in each camp, so didn't that make you the ultimate insider?

Using my outsider advantage has been key to most of my successes, but I've learned that it's not always clear to people why. The benefits of being an *insider* seem obvious, but it's only when you start looking for the advantages in being an outsider that they start to jump out at you. What are they?

1. As an outsider, you bring a fresh perspective and the freedom to apply it. Just by coming into a situation from the outside, you're not going to be in the habit of seeing things the way people there usually see them. Exactly because you were elsewhere until now, you aren't attached to that history of "how it's always been done." Sometimes just having that freshness of perspective lets you see valuable alternatives that others have been missing because they were too close to see anything new.

2. When you're an outsider, people don't know what to expect—so they have to listen. People can't pigeonhole you or dismiss your ideas because they don't know, yet, what you're all about. While they're trying to figure you out, they have to open their minds, at least partway. They can't just say, "Oh, him. Never mind about him, he's been in this business for a long time; he's just a such-and-such."

3. As an outsider, you have more freedom to act. Along

with creative freedom, being an outsider means you have emotional freedom: you don't feel obliged to do things the way
they've always been done. I like to say that I can impact a situation if it didn't have an impact on me. I mean that if I'm an
insider, and the place where I'm trying to work is the place that
gave me my start and my friendships and my way of life, then
I'm going to have a lot of obligations and debts. Think about
the *Godfather* movies, or any of the more realistic accounts
of the Mafia. You can picture those big gatherings where the
members of the community come to pay their respects to the
head of the family. They kneel and kiss his ring. That kind of
obligation, to pay tribute to the people who've always been in
charge and to do things the way they've always been done, is
very limiting. When I worked in gospel, or racing, or any of
the places I've had success, I didn't have to kiss anyone's ring
because I wasn't an insider to begin with. When I wanted to try
something new, I wasn't risking my position or my standing in
the community—because I wasn't from the community. I was
just a newcomer with something to offer.

I benefited from all three of these advantages when I became president of DEI and started to work on the company's relationships with
its corporate sponsors. As I discovered right away, there was one set
way of doing things across the industry. Why were they set in their
ways? NASCAR had enjoyed a tremendous amount of growth in commercial support over the years, which had been a great thing for the
sport and for the fans, but exactly because they were used to success,
there weren't a lot of people thinking about new approaches. When
I arrived, growth in the industry had leveled off, and it was time for
some fresh ideas, but the requests for proposals that I was seeing were
still all very similar.

The idea of how a sponsor could benefit from supporting a team
was that the team would put the sponsor's logo on the race car and

then do their best to win or run at the front of the pack. That way people would see that logo on television and in publicity photos of the car. That's a great model, but it was pretty much the only model at the time, which meant that every team was competing to give their sponsor the same thing: a winning car that would spend a lot of time up front, where the television cameras would see it.

But I wasn't in the habit of working that way, and I wasn't emotionally committed to doing things how they were "always" done. I felt freer to ask each sponsor or potential sponsor: What are your specific objectives? What kind of return would you most like to see on your investment in my company, and how could we help you get that? I didn't feel so attached to the way things had been done before, so I could see it a little differently and I could feel comfortable trying something new.

Plus, when I started taking some new approaches, neither my company nor our sponsors could tune me out because they had heard it all from me before. They actually had to listen to me to find out who they were dealing with. And once we asked our new questions, we found that our different sponsors actually had very different goals. Sure, some wanted their logos seen on television to make their brands look bigger. But others wanted to increase foot traffic to their stores. The U.S. Army, which was a DEI sponsor, wanted to encourage people to consider the armed services as an alternative career. There was a wide range of goals.

For one sponsor, I said, "Forget putting logos on winning cars for a minute. Have you ever thought about the fact that we have a database of five million race fans, and that you might get more bang for your buck by marketing directly to our fan list? What if we sent text messages to fans with coupons they could bring to the store for team-themed products?" Now, if you come from an industry that already markets in this way, that idea was hardly rocket science. But it took an outsider's fresh perspective to see that opportunity in racing.

With gospel artists, too, I've been able to help them succeed because I wasn't loyal to the established way of doing things. Not having to do things the old way or kiss anyone's ring freed me to do something people in the faith-based community tended not to do: talk about business. Now, if you're not from the church community, you may not realize what a foreign idea worldly business can be. So let me tell you, I can't count all the times gospel people have said to me that "business concerns have no place in spiritual life or spiritual work." Our industry might be the "Christian music business," but many people lose sight of the fact that it is, after all, *business*. Of course, gospel people need money like anyone else, but when they run short they're liable to say, "It doesn't matter. I can pray through it." Now, that's a powerful attitude, a lifesaver sometimes. But other times it's just too limiting. I know that when a singer or a minister can keep a roof over his head and feed his family, he or she has *more* time and focus for God's work, not less. And as they say, faith without works is dead. So instead of seeing the music business and church business as irreconcilable opposites, I see them as opposites that attract, and I try to help them settle down together and get married. That has been the intention of "About My Father's Business," the conference I helped create to bring the best of the gospel world together in Indianapolis so we can meet, reenergize, learn from each other, and lift each other up.

WHAT ABOUT INSIDER ADVANTAGE?

BUT WAIT. ISN'T THERE an advantage to being an insider? Of course there is, some of the time, but in the global business environment, playing the insider is limiting both for individuals and for organizations. Let me explain. I remember attending a dinner once and hearing a corporate representative talk about his company's commitment to diversity. He said that his company "understood that people feel more comfortable doing business with people who look like them." For that reason, he said, when his company opened a new office, they made it their policy to hire people from the local community. Now, that's all fine as far as it goes—I'm always happy to hear that companies are looking for talent in the local communities where they operate. But what happens when some of those "people who look like the local community" turn out to be good at their jobs and worthy of promotion? What happens when some of them turn out to have skills and ideas that could benefit other parts of the company, in other parts of town or of the country or the world where people look a little different? Wouldn't it be better for everyone if those people could go as far as their talents and skills could take them, rather than remaining limited to the places where they "look like the local community"?

That's the problem with the insider approach: it shuts you in. But I've learned that in some situations where I don't look like I fit in, where I'm obviously an outsider, I can be comfortable and content. When I showed up for work the first day at Dale Earnhardt Inc., there were four hundred employees in the company and not a single one besides me was African-American. So there I was, the one black face in the entire company, but after a few weeks my wife said to me: "You know, Max, you're happier here than you've been in a lot of places."

Why was that? It comes down to the values and the lifestyle of the people I found at DEI and in racing overall. First, racing people are there because they love it. They've built their lives and their work around their passion, which is what I have always tried to do, too. Their commitment and their enthusiasm came through to me in the way they did their jobs, and that made me feel at home. Second, racing people are family people. They travel from track to track together with their families and often nurture their children in the family business. That's a way of life very close to mine. Third, I felt at home with the Christian values of the people I met. Racing is the only major sport where there is an official prayer before the start of competition, and you can feel the influence of the church in the way people conduct themselves. Finally, when it came to all my practical questions as I got started in a new job in a new part of the country, I found that the people I met were open with me and willing to share information. I could ask them, What do I need to know? And when they saw that I shared their feeling for racing, they opened up to me and told me. It's hard to imagine how I could have felt more welcome than I did.

WE ARE ALL OUTSIDERS SOME OF THE TIME

IN THE RANGE OF experiences different people have, from feeling more often the insider to more often the outsider, I suppose I'm pretty close to the extreme. I've been an outsider most of my life. For me, always being the outsider meant that I needed to learn to sense when the people around me had also experienced life as the outsider, because that might be all I could find that would let me connect with them. As I got better at connecting with people based on their outsider experiences, I discovered something I hadn't known. There is so much variety in America, so many different groups each with their own ways, that at some point everyone feels like the outsider. The day comes when you feel you're too fat or too skinny; you went to public or private school when it should have been the other way around; you're too much of a nerd or too much of a jock; your politics are too this or too that. It happens to everyone, that moment when you feel in the pit of your stomach that you've been pushed to the outside, alone, set apart as if we weren't all made in God's image.

If that doesn't sound like an advantage, you're right. It isn't. But that unhappy experience is an opportunity to develop a very powerful perspective, which is to recognize that as an outsider you can do what I described above: see a situation differently from the way insiders are used to seeing it, require people's attention because they don't know what to make of you, and act with greater freedom because you're not beholden to the powers that be. I remember one evening after my son, who was seven at the time, came home from a golf lesson. He said he hated golf. What was wrong? He was ugly, he told Jennifer and me. And he hated his feet.

What was going on?

It turned out some other kids at the golf lesson had been making remarks about his color. You might think that in the era of Tiger Woods this sort of thing wouldn't happen anymore, but indeed someone had called him "chocolate." Then someone told him that his feet looked like poop. And on it went. He came home and said he hated the color of his feet and he never wanted to go outside again.

Well. It wasn't as if this was the first time someone ever made remarks about color. I asked my son, "Tell me something. Do you think your mom is beautiful?"

He didn't really feel like talking, but I pushed him: "Do you?"

He said yeah, Mom was beautiful.

"What about your dad? Is he a handsome man?"

He said yes.

I said, "We're brown, too, right?"

And so we talked and he found his way back to seeing with his own eyes and making his own judgments. It was a chance to discover how being made to feel like you are the outsider was a lesson in learning to follow your own compass, to trust in your own perspective. I've found that the people who move forward and excel are the ones who've taken in those lessons, who move to the beat of their own drum and let their own light shine.

Not long after, I told the story of these other children's slurs to an adult friend, the mother of a child we know. They're a white family, Catholic. She told me, "Kids can be mean sometimes. It's just kids being kids." She was trying to be empathetic, I knew, but she was minimizing what had happened. "It was just teasing," she said. "It didn't mean anything." She said we shouldn't let it bother us.

Then a few weeks later she called me up, practically in tears. It turned out that her son, who attended an expensive private school, was being excluded by the other boys who used to be his friends. They were all white and they were all affluent, but her son was the only Catholic, and the other boys had told him that he wasn't a real Christian because he wasn't born again. Now he couldn't be part of their clique. When she called me, she nearly had a meltdown apologizing. She said she hadn't known what a parent goes through until their own child is the one excluded. And so there it was: maybe for the first time, she was in an environment where she expected to fit in, but now she and her son were the outsiders.

When I talk about the outsider advantage, I don't mean that I think these experiences are all for the best. And let's be honest: having the experience of being an outsider, whether once or many times, guarantees nothing—not understanding, not success, not becoming a nicer person. But while it's no guarantee, it is an opportunity to develop the skill set I'm describing in this chapter, which might be the most vital skill set there is for the twenty-first century. Let me describe for you now how to build these skills.

DON'T TRY TO BE A CHAMELEON

THE FIRST STEP, IN my experience, is to stop trying to fit in by copying the people you're trying to succeed with and passing yourself off as one of them. For a lot of people, fitting in is habit—they've spent a lot of time trying to be successful chameleons. I understand that pressure because I've felt it almost everywhere I've been, even when I've been the person in charge. When I became chief of global operations for DEI, I came down from Indiana to North Carolina and joined the company as the only person of color in an industry with the reputation of being Southern and white. That was intimidating in itself, but in addition I was coming from the music industry, so racing people kept asking me, in more and less subtle ways, "Do you really know what you're getting yourself into?" Now, I didn't share their skepticism, but I understood it. If I wasn't one of them and I didn't know racing, which was the very center of their lives, how could I know what mattered most to them? How could I take care of them?

In those first days down in Charlotte, I remember thinking back to my neighborhood as a teenager, after I had promised myself I would make a better life by working with anyone around me who could help. Back then, I knew that before I could do anything else, I would have to have the respect of a crew—not really a gang, but a group of serious troublemakers. To get that respect—what we now call *street cred*—I thought at first that I would have to blend in like a chameleon, looking and acting just like the rest of the crew, staying out all night with my wild cousin and his boys, doing the kind of crazy, stupid things that got young men hurt or jailed. And yet I also knew that wasn't for me. How could I get the respect of this crew without getting drawn into self-destructive foolishness that could keep me from ever reaching my goals?

All I could do to begin was to get to know what made them tick. And as I did, I realized they didn't need me to do everything just like they did. They only needed me to show my respect for what they felt and who they were. So I stayed out late with my wild cousin and his troublemaking friends, but before I slipped out to meet them, I would finish my homework. And though I stayed out very late, I would get home while my mother was still asleep—not two days later, when she would have been frantic. I still had some time for baseball and wrestling and playing the drums, and for school work, too.

Of course, pretty soon some of my new "troublemaking" friends started to notice that I was still going to school and getting good grades. And here was what surprised me: it turned out I wasn't the only one with multiple interests. I wasn't the only one hoping to fit in some achievement at school or on the wrestling mat along with the wild nights. It turned out that others in the group saw the benefit in having me live this compromise. Some of them started doing it as well. That was when I realized it might be possible to have street cred and academic cred and on-the-job cred—and most important, how to exist in all of these worlds simultaneously: not by imitating the others, but by showing respect for what mattered to them while interesting them in what mattered to me.

That was the insight I brought with me when I started to work at DEI. I knew the team was never going to think I was Southern or white. There was no trick to make them believe I had spent my whole life in racing. But that was all right, because I wasn't trying to be a chameleon; I was trying to show my respect for what mattered to them. The only way to do that was to put in the time to listen. So when I joined DEI and started traveling on the road from race to race, even though there was a space for me on the owner's Lear jet, I flew with the team on the team plane. Every day when I went to the track, I didn't wear a three-piece suit; I wore the team competition uniform. I wanted the whole company to see I wasn't just the "suit" from management; I was part of the team. I spent a lot of my down time with them, eating and drinking and talking, hearing their concerns and finding out what was really going on with the company. And by spending my time with them, I was letting them know that while I might have a different background and a different job than they had, I didn't think I was any greater than they were. I was showing them that I wanted to help them do their jobs better.

After a while, someone passed on a compliment that made me know I was getting through. It was something one of the mechanics had told him: "You know, Max isn't one of us—but he's one of us." That's when I knew I could make it in racing.

BECOME AN AMBASSADOR

IT'S ONLY WHEN YOU stop trying to blend in that you can make use of the advantages of being an outsider. When you can present yourself by saying, honestly, yes, I'm not from here, I'm not just like you, and I may not yet understand what you need, so tell me. Tell me everything I need to know. We're different, but we can find a way to understand each other and work together. When you take that stance, presenting yourself openly as the outsider, then differences and even "problems" can turn out to be unexpected resources. When I first met Dale Junior, we had a legal negotiation to resolve, but what helped us to connect as people, and to establish the basic trust that let us work together, was sharing our experiences as kids of divorce, and our relationships with our stepmothers. When I met Tony Gwynn, he needed new representation, but everyone knew that. What let us connect was that I found the experience we had in common: we had both been betrayed by people close to us, and lived through times when it was hard for either of us to trust anyone. These disadvantages, these hard times in our past, became the resource we drew on to connect and succeed together.

I'M MENTIONING THESE EXAMPLES again to make clear what they all have in common: they were all challenging experiences from my past that had nothing to do with the "official" business I was working on. But they had everything to do with showing the person I wanted to work with that, although I might be an outsider in some ways, I could understand the things that concerned them most.

You get the outsider advantage, in other words, by doing two things. First, as I've said, you resist the pressure to try to blend in like a chameleon, and instead you present yourself frankly as an outsider. That positions you to make your best use of the first four rules in this book.

1. An outsider knows he isn't a native to the situation he's in today, and that means he doesn't always know how things are done or what really moves people and shapes their decisions in this place—so he *listens and observes* not just to advance his own agenda but to understand what makes them tick.

2. An outsider has to find the overlap between his goals and the goals of those he wants to work with—seeing where he and they want to be, not just where they are.

3. An outsider doesn't have access to an insider network, so he has to appreciate each person he meets on his or her own terms.

4. An outsider can't count on people working with him or taking him seriously out of tradition, habit, or familiarity. He has to show those he wants to work with what's in it for them.

But while getting the outsider advantage is a continuation of my principles, it's also an expansion of those principles to a bigger stage, where the number of people you can help to connect and succeed grows exponentially. Now you go beyond connecting with others one-on-one. You offer yourself as an ambassador, a go-between who helps two or more other people or groups to find the common ground where they can work together profitably in ways they couldn't without you.

• •

Your Mission as Ambassador:
Seven Steps to Mutual Benefit

1. Get to know each side separately. Establish comfort and trust by listening to understand and showing your common points of connection. Each side has to feel that they can talk to you, that you hear and respect their concerns, and also that you are not so loyal to the other side that you are compromised. You can't move forward until you establish basic comfort and trust.

2. Learn what each side wants and what they lack. What are they trying to do? What are their obstacles? What stands in their way? What are their fears? Show them that you see where they want to be.

3. Find the areas where their interests overlap. Before they can work together usefully, someone needs to appreciate each side for how they could each help the other succeed. Become the person who appreciates how well they could work together. Use the freshness of your outsider perspective and your freedom to try things that are different from how it's usually done.

4. Get to know the terms each side uses to express its goals and its situation. Those terms might be financial or artistic, spiritual or personal, or something else. They may seem reasonable to you or not, but that doesn't matter. You have to be able to talk to each side in the terms that make sense to them.

5. Explain what each side wants in the other one's terms. If side A wants financial gain and side B wants to be true to its artistic vision, then you have to explain to the finance side that the people at B will help them reach their financial goals. At the same time, you have to explain to the artists how side A will help them reach their artistic goals. In other words, translate each side's goals into the other's way of talking.

6. Help revise their plan for working together by translating their ongoing negotiations into the terms they understand. If talks break down, remind each side how the other can still help them reach their goals.

7. Don't overreach. Don't set yourself up as the expert who knows everything about each side. Your role as the ambassador is to establish trust and to translate goals and proposals so that people can work together. It's not to try to make people understand each other completely. Don't try to bring about universal understanding and harmony. Part of the outsider advantage is understanding something that not everyone gets: people really are different from one another. And that's fine. We can do great work together without

being exactly alike or having a perfect understanding—
which is good, because down here on Earth we're not going
to get a perfect understanding any time soon. But we can
still make it work. Keep the spotlight off yourself and deliver
your messages.

· ‚ ·

THE OUTSIDER ADVANTAGE IN A CONFLICT

OFFERING YOURSELF AS AMBASSADOR works in formal
business situations, informal personal situations, and everything in
between. It has made my career, and more than once it has saved my
hide. I remember one incident in southern California. It was six in
the morning on race day, and it felt like it was two hundred degrees
already at the track. We had a little time, so my public relations guy at
DEI, Blair, said we should go get a cup of coffee. We drove to a Star-
bucks forty miles away from the track and got in line. That's when I
noticed a bunch of men all dressed in red, pointing me out to each
other and looking me over. These looks were not friendly. The whole
situation felt like some gang thing on the street, but these were white
guys dressed head-to-toe in red, Budweiser-logo racing apparel. They
had the t-shirts and the polo shirts, the bank cap and the pit hat—one
of them was even wearing the red leather uniform jacket, though it
was already very, very hot there in Southern California. I couldn't see
how that was going to be good for his mood.

Before I knew it one of the guys in red is in front of me and he's
angry. He says, "You don't know what the —— you're doing, keeping the eight! You're screwing up the legacy!" I felt like telling him,
"Dude, lighten up. It's not even seven in the morning. I haven't even
had my coffee yet." But he was too angry; a joke might only have made
him angrier. He was going off, right in my face, and he had five of his
friends coming toward us now. They were all wearing their red Bud-

weiser clothes with Junior's old number eight, the number Junior had worn when he raced with DEI, the number that DEI hadn't let him take with him to his new team.

Blair was getting nervous. He leaned in and said to me, quietly, "We've got to go." But this man wearing the number eight was still yelling. And the worst part of all of this was, I had been warned. The fans loved Junior so much, and they have such strong feelings about the Earnhardt family, that when he left the team and we kept the rights to the number eight, NASCAR sent a representative to tell me to get executive protection. I remember at the time I said, essentially, "Huh? What is 'executive protection?'" A bodyguard, it turned out.

The concern was that some fans might want to do me harm because we kept the rights to the number eight car, and so all the Dale Earnhardt Jr. fan merchandise which bore his number was no longer accurate. That was when I hired Sarge. But I hadn't wanted to bother Sarge over a cup of coffee at six in the morning, so he was still back at the track, forty miles away. Blair and I were on our own.

"Do you have any idea what you've done?" the first guy in red yelled. "I've got $50,000 worth of . . . *do you have any idea?*"

It seemed the more he realized that he was actually talking to someone responsible, the madder he got. He wanted to do something with all that disappointment, all that frustration that had been festering over the past months. He wanted a fight.

"Listen!" I told him. "I love Junior. I wish he hadn't left."

That seemed to get his attention.

"I'm telling you, I feel the same way as you," I said. If I had anything going for me at that moment, it was that I was an outsider. He didn't know what to expect of me. That meant there was a chance some part of his mind was still open, and he might notice what I actually said and did, not just whatever he expected of the man who let Junior go.

"I totally respect the legacy," I told him. "Believe me, I appreciate what you lost. I wish he had stayed, too."

I was trying to show him that I understood his feelings. How sacred it was to him. How passionate he felt. And now, instead of yelling some more, he looked at me again. They all looked at me. I hoped they were trying out the idea that maybe we weren't enemies.

He said, "I even got the new train! Have you got the new train?"

"I don't have the train," I said. "You have the train?"

"Man I wish he could have kept the eight. My wife . . . hey, can she have your autograph?"

And then I knew it was all right. We could do something else with all that frustration and disappointment that he had wanted to take out on me. We could share it. We all missed Junior. We all wished it could have gone another way. I signed the autograph for this fan's wife. Once again, I wasn't one of them—but I was one of them.

What made these guys tick was their racing way of life. The benefit to them was to keep that way of life going, and though it had seemed like I was a threat to it, I was able to change the direction so that our conversation helped nurture that way of life. The autograph did the same thing. I realized that although they weren't a gang, still, like gang members they wanted respect; they wanted their concerns understood; they wanted to be taken seriously. And although there may have been six of them facing me and Blair, they must have felt powerless—they had lost Junior and their clothes were out of date and they must have been afraid the thing they loved and invested in was being taken away.

I got back to the track and everything was okay, except that I had to face Sarge and tell him that I sneaked off without him. He looked down at me and said, "Come on! My first time to shine on the job and you leave me?" I told him I had learned my lesson.

HOW THE OUTSIDER ADVANTAGE BUILT NASCAR

THE POWER OF THE outsider advantage brings success not just to individuals, but to organizations and even whole industries. In fact, I would say it built NASCAR. Of course, by now stock car racing is a national phenomenon. It has grown to become the second most popular professional sport after football, as measured by television ratings. Of the top-twenty-attended sporting events in the United States, NASCAR holds seventeen. The seventy five million fans spend over three billion dollars a year on sales of NASCAR-licensed products. More Fortune 500 companies sponsor it than any other sport. And yet what people don't realize, when they contemplate all this success, is that it all began with local get-togethers where people would show up to race their own cars. Even as it grew, the team owners who built the sport into a phenomenon didn't have a formal background in either business administration or competitive sports. Not at all. For the most part they were, and still are, business outsiders. What they had going for them was their passion for racing and their understanding of the audience, which they knew because they were part of it themselves. That connection to the fans led them to do things much differently from other sports.

For example, when people who are only familiar with other professional sports come to their first race, they're often surprised to realize that we're not selling hot dogs or beer. In fact, not only are the food and beverage concessions very limited (mostly to things that cool you off on a hot day), we also let people bring in all the coolers that they want. That's because someone who understood what matters to the fans realized a long time ago that if you let folks bring in their own food and drink, they'll stay longer.

Unlike other sports, NASCAR comes to town like a traveling circus—it only happens once a year, so fans don't want to miss any of it. Most make it a family vacation. The race is part of a whole week of activities; the week is part of an ongoing way of life. So fans come for a week, visit the track every day, and all week long they're buying merchandise they'll use all year. With fans coming for the week, we couldn't even keep up with the beer demand if we tried. It's good for them and it's good for business—the average fan spends nearly a thousand dollars, and that doesn't include hotel or travel.

Another surprise is that you can meet every single driver. The garages and haulers where the crews and drivers work, and where they wait before the race begins, are open to the fans. It's as if you went to a ball game and found Michael Jordan walking around in the crowd before the game. Visiting the haulers is like being able to walk into the locker room. The press, too, has a huge amount of access, and so there is far more unfiltered information available than in other sports. In all these ways, racing is unusually open to its fans. They wait for drivers to walk by on the way to the garage or to the prerace meeting with the officials, and call out questions or take their pictures. The drivers expect this, and they respond.

As NASCAR continued to grow, it was necessary to institute some "back to basics" initiatives to make sure the expansion of the sport wasn't interfering with that core lifestyle on which the whole sport and its success was built. One element is Christian worship. As I've mentioned, racing is the only sport where you see a prayer on television before the race starts. Historically, fans woke up on Sunday morning, went to church, ate their after-church meal, and then settled in to watch a race. But as the sport spread across the country, the scheduled start times for races out west got out of sync with people's schedules for church and their Sunday meal. In time, the governing body recognized the problem and changed California start time so most people across the country could experience the race in the way they preferred. They understood that the drivers and crews and fans are the real insiders of NASCAR, the ones to whom the NASCAR owners and governing body must listen to understand, so the sport can continue its amazing success. It's success that came from a group of outsiders who weren't worried about how a professional sport was run in other places; they were just concerned with respecting their audience and speaking their language. That was NASCAR's outsider advantage.

• • • • •   CHAPTER SIX   • • • • •

Gather **Your** Inner **Circle**

RESUMES CAN FOOL YOU. Look at mine today and you might think I had some master plan I followed, step by logical step, blending entrepreneurship and law to reach a leadership position in a major sport. But as I always tell people, when I got started I didn't know what the heck I was doing. Instead, two things guided me to success. First were these rules I'm sharing with you now. Second was a group of loyal and talented people I've been blessed to know, people who treated my success and well-being like it was their own: my inner circle.

These people I refer to as my inner circle have provided the support, insight, honesty, and guidance that have made it possible to realize my dreams—and then some. They are people whose connections to me go much deeper than any one project or goal. I have been fortunate in my inner circle, but everyone has the makings of a powerful inner circle among the people they already know, whether family, friends, colleagues, or mentors. It's a question of learning to tap into their true potential.

One of the most important people for me, someone who helped make possible many of my proudest achievements, was Reggie White, the great defensive lineman for the Philadelphia Eagles and the Green Bay Packers. I became his agent, and in time he helped me get to know the most important people in NASCAR, but the truth is that when we met, neither of us was talking about racing. We weren't even talking about football. I want to tell the story of how my inner circle grew, and how he came to be part of it, because that had to happen before I could even begin to get where I am today. The story begins long before I met Reggie White.

Back in Indianapolis when I was a teenager, I was friends with a boy whose father took an interest in me because we both loved sports, especially baseball. Back then, I had no one to come to my games and cheer me on. My father had passed away, my stepfather wasn't interested, and my mother had a house full of kids to manage. Somehow, Uncle Ronald, as we kids called him, took me in. Even on Saturday mornings, after he might have had too many beers on Friday night, he would still be at my game. He talked to me about my playing and my potential, and praised me because I wasn't "all slang-talking," as he said. He told me he admired me for conducting myself in a way that was "businesslike and respectable." Acting as a kind of father figure, he encouraged me at every game. He told me I had the potential to go pro, and when I was offered a scholarship to Notre Dame, no one was happier. When I came back to Indianapolis to visit, I always called him. To this day, he says I might have had the potential to play in the major leagues, before the injury in college that put an end to my days as a ballplayer.

What it meant for me to have Uncle Ronald in my inner circle had two parts. First, it was support and encouragement I could count on, especially when I needed to play my best. I've come to see that I have two extremes in my personality; I have very thick armor, but once you penetrate this armor, I'm very sensitive. So I've always set very high standards. I'm my own worst critic as I work to be pleasing to God and to my family. But I'm a human being, too. I need that time with people who have my best interests at heart, people with whom I don't have to worry about another agenda, because I know that they care about me.

The second blessing I found with Uncle Ronald, and in the rest of my inner circle since then, was honest feedback from those who see more in me, at times, than I can. That's what makes an inner circle so powerful: the combination of support without any strings attached and honest feedback you can trust.

START CLOSE TO HOME

FOR MOST PEOPLE IT begins with a close friend or a family member. My wife's inner circle began with her sister, who is her best friend. What matters is that it's someone with no other agenda than focusing on your progress as an individual. My mother became another of the early and important people in my inner circle. From early on, we had an unusual relationship because I hadn't seen her for seven years after my father took me away. When I came back home my relationship with her was difficult. In my heart, I always felt the bond with her, but I had left when I was a boy and I came back as a teenager. It was very awkward at first, but in time it meant she could be more like a friend to me than if I had been home in the usual way. She had limited education, but she was wise, candid, and outspoken. I always knew she would give it to me straight. She was the one who showed me how people would open up to you, whether the mayor or the local drug addict, if you showed you were interested in whatever made them tick. She made people feel comfortable and secure and everybody told her their business, and in this way she got an education in relationships that you couldn't get at any school. I relied on her for that understanding as I started to launch my career.

Out of college, I worked for General Motors in a college-grad-in-training program. They identified me as a "high-potential candidate" and put me in a fast-track program. On my evaluations, I always got four out of four. Then I ran into a supervisor a few years older than me, and suddenly with her I couldn't do anything right. She told me I had no communication skills. She told me my work was poor. I tried to talk it out with her and I got nowhere. This was probably the first time I had run into a problem with someone in authority that I couldn't talk my way through. My work suffered. I became depressed. I told my mother I was ready to quit—I had several different offers out of college, and I thought I might try another company.

My mother had no corporate experience—she had worked as a singer and a nurse—but she knew about people and their ways. She told me, no, you're not going to quit. You leave on your own terms—don't let anyone drive you away. Because in every job you ever have, you'll encounter that same difficult boss, just with a different name and face.

I wasn't happy with her advice, but I knew it came from her pure desire for my success. So I decided to stick it out. Slowly I learned to work with that supervisor, and though it was never smooth or enjoyable, I wound up being promoted to district sales manager. I did quit, eventually, but I left on my own terms. And sure enough, when I got other jobs, now and then I had a similar difficulty with a supervisor, only I was in higher positions and the supervisor was a whole lot more important. But by the time I encountered those challenges, they were easier to take. I could better tolerate the criticism, and I knew how to make myself necessary to the supervisor and to the company. I think it became easier thanks to the maturity I had gained by taking my mother's advice and sticking with that first job.

THE FOUNDATION IS TRUST

YOUR INNER CIRCLE IS your source for unconditional support and objective feedback; it's also your help in regaining your personal focus and resolve when they start to waver. It may be the most valuable resource anyone has. How do you build your inner circle? Of course, you want the most insightful and experienced people you can find, but to begin, put all career calculations aside. Just like building a house, you have to start with a strong foundation or it doesn't much matter what you put on top. The foundation of your inner circle, whether your concerns have to do with work, home, or spirit, is the same: trust. Find those people whose honesty, care, and commitment to your long-term success are as strong as your dedication to theirs. People who are like family—even if, like me, your family didn't always act "like family." Look for the people around you who treat you the way family *should* do, and then make sure you do the same.

Maybe you already have an inner circle that works for you in just the way I've described. In that case you are blessed indeed. But if as you read this you need to gather an inner circle around you for the first time, or if you need to reconsider whether the people who fill this role for you are still suited to your life situation and your career challenges today, let me offer a few suggestions. Let's begin as if you have never had an inner circle, and you would like now to get started.

List your candidates.

Make a list of the people you have gone to for advice and help, whether recently or in the past. Consider every area of your life. It's not as easy as it seems; you may need to come back to the list over a few days. Just keep writing down names.

Cast a wide net.

The only mistake at this stage is not being open-minded enough. Here are some things that are *not* required for members of your inner circle:

- They don't need to be your closest family or the friends you see every day.
- It doesn't matter what they do for a living or how much money they make.
- They don't need to have formal education.

- They don't need to be famous or powerful.
- They don't need to be any particular age.
- They don't need to work in your industry.

Include people you don't always agree with.

It's all right if you don't always get along with the people in your inner circle. In fact, as I'll explain, people you can argue with—respectfully and thoughtfully, without anyone holding a grudge in the end—are some of the most helpful people there are.

Go for straight trust.

What you need is people who have never betrayed you, who will take your side unconditionally and tell you the truth, whether you like it or not. The most important test is trust: once you have your list, go through it name by name and cross off everyone, even friends and family, who don't pass that test. If they are prone to see your success as their loss, or if they have put their own interests ahead of yours, even some of the time, then although they may be important people whom you will love for your entire life, cross them off this list.

To help as you draw up your list and then whittle it down until there's nothing but trust, here are some questions to help you picture each relationship clearly. Ask yourself:

- How long have you known this person? In what different capacities? Consider each one.
- Are they calming? Do they reduce your stress or add to it?
- Do you respect this person? Is the respect mutual?
- Do you call them because you think they'll have good insight?
- Have you found that you could use and trust their advice?
- Even if you are not always in touch, does the relationship keep growing?
- Have you had disagreements and worked through them?
- Are you both willing to agree to disagree?

Cut down your list until you feel certain about everyone on it.

You can have a big group, but you only need two to start, so be choosy. It's better to have fewer people in your inner circle than to have someone who may be undermining or unworthy of your trust—even once in a while. Not sure about a name on your list? Then the answer is no. He or she may still be a good person, someone who will always be a part of your life, but not in this role.

As your list grows shorter, there will be close friends and family members who don't make the cut. You may also find that someone who remains on the list has been out of your life too long. All this is valuable information. Keep cutting until you feel certain about the names that are left—again, one is too few, but two is enough.

How can you be certain you have the right people? I would like to give you the formula—exactly how to recognize what you need for your inner circle in others, and how to provide what they need in return—but there is no formula. It's something you have to learn by feel, from the examples of the best people in your life. So as part of this exercise, let me tell a story about recognizing a key member of my inner circle where I didn't expect to find him.

This was in the days after my father died and I was living with my sister Traci in Nevada, supposedly in the care of my stepmother but mostly on our own. Thanks to news of his funeral, my mother finally located Traci and me in Las Vegas, where my father had hidden us away from her. Now she made arrangements for us to fly back to Indianapolis to rejoin her family.

It was just the two of us kids on that airplane and neither of us wanted to go. As bad as things might have gotten for us, our life with our stepmother was what we were used to, and we didn't want to leave it. But my mother had come to Las Vegas and made it clear that no one had a choice.

When we walked off the plane there seemed to be an ocean of people at the gate, people in all shapes, sizes, ages, and colors, waiting for us. It was frightening. We were supposed to be related to all of them, but my sister didn't recognize a soul, and many were strangers to me, too. This wasn't the kind of reunion where people were calling out to each other and hugging, full of joy. It was quiet. Tears were falling.

All those people who met us at the airport followed us home. The house—our house, now—was very small, two bedrooms for seven people, and we had a baby half-brother we had never met, and I think we both felt very alone. Finally, Traci began to feel some familiarity around our older half-brother, Jerry. He had often looked after us, the designated babysitter, before we were taken away. Jerry was the most levelheaded, calm, clear sibling, even in the times of hostility—the emotional glue that had held the family together. After my father took us away to Las Vegas, we missed him as much as anyone.

Now he sat on the couch with us, speaking to us again as he used to do in his soft voice and showing his heartfelt smile. Traci thought she might remember that smile. That night Jerry stayed up with us very late, until everybody else had gone to bed. When it was finally quiet, he sat with us on the couch, me on one side and Traci on the other. That's when he brought out the letters. He had written them to us when we were gone, saying how much he missed us and how he didn't want us to think that nobody cared that we had been taken away. He kept them so he could show us the postmarks on the envelopes, and how they had all come back to him stamped with "addressee unknown," "return to sender," and so forth. The letters were his way to prove that he never stopped trying to find us. He had taken our disappearance very hard.

Jerry read us the letters and we sat on the couch together and cried. We fell asleep there, my head on one of Jerry's shoulders and Traci's on the other. It was the first time that place felt anything like a home. I don't think my mother could have been happier or more relieved to have us back, or that she could have tried harder to make things right, but it was Jerry who first made himself our ally, who helped us find our place again and began to stitch our torn family back together. He became a model for me of what an ally should be, a true member of my inner circle, and ever since I've looked for those qualities of dedication and honesty, and that sense that we stand or fall together.

MAKING THE MOST OF YOUR INNER CIRCLE

ONCE YOU HAVE YOUR list of people you know you can trust and benefit from having in your inner circle, you need to start making more use of this extraordinary resource. That means a conscious choice to reach out more often. These are the people who get you the most, so if you're not in the habit of speaking to them, start finding the time. Get out your calendar. Pick up the phone. If you already speak to them often, be sure that you find opportunities to go beyond the usual banter and hanging out, so you can talk about the things that make you both tick. I'm not saying you need to go all serious on them and start asking formally for their advice. With some people, you do that, but with others you just talk, and no one can really say what part of the conversation is advice and what's mentoring and what's just hanging out talking about life. All that matters is that you each listen to understand what moves the other. The result is any number of benefits. To make the most of them:

- **Check in often, and make sure you can really talk.** Part of the benefit of having an inner circle is that there are people who support you, who know the important things going on in your life and the things you wish for in the future. So make sure you have the chance to let them know. Sometimes you may not realize you're asking for help until they hear you struggling. You may not realize you have a question until you hear the answer they're offering. Again, you have selected these relationships because they're already so good; you don't need to reengineer them, you just need to tend to them. That might mean spending more time alone with each other. It might mean recognizing that some of the people you enjoy spending time with prevent you from talking about the things that matter most to you, and then finding time away from those distracting people, even if you enjoy them.

- **Allow the people you can trust to support and insulate you.** Few of us can show our true feelings all of the time, and maintaining the appropriate face for the work world or for the people who depend on us takes its toll. With your inner circle, you can be honest about how you feel and know that you won't get taken advantage of by someone with another agenda.

- **Listen for wisdom even from people who don't have formal learning or specialized knowledge of your field.** The power of your inner circle grows out of its members' concern for you and their knowledge of your ways. That means that they may have insight even about situations that they do not formally understand.

My brothers and sister used to joke about my musical ability, or rather my lack of it. Everyone in my family had musical talent, and I did play drums for a while, but sometimes my brothers would laugh and say, "Uh-oh. Max is going to have to find something else to do with himself." They were just teasing, but there was wisdom in it. One of the greatest gifts in my life turned out to be knowing what I didn't know and what God didn't mean for me to do. I don't sing, I don't dance, and I don't act. I have worked with artists all my life, but I'm not an artist. I'm grateful my family helped show me where my talents lay.

Sometimes my wife will hear me on a business call, and afterward she'll tell me: "Your delivery's off." She means that even though she doesn't know anything about the content of my conversation, she can recognize the sound of my voice when

I'm focused and persuasive—and what she just heard wasn't it. Her feedback is my cue to reconsider my goals and what might be keeping me from feeling more at ease and effective—more myself—so I can reach them.

Sometimes people in my inner circle can see a problem I'm having by the way it shows in my face or as tension I carry in my body. Again, they may only be able to say, "What's the matter? Why is your forehead all wrinkled up?" or, "You don't seem right today." Sometimes even my kids have seen it. That may not sound like much to go on, but I've learned over the years to look for the connections between the mistakes I make and the stress people close to me can see me carrying in my body before I go wrong. When I'm pushing too hard to save a relationship that's already past saving, for example, I tense up. I hate to let a relationship go—I value people so much. I'll just keep trying to make it work until someone in my inner circle gives me this kind of feedback. That helps me to remind myself: if it feels this wrong, something isn't right. Maybe this relationship can't be fixed. Maybe I have to stop pushing and cut my losses. Of course, for you the difficult area may not be relationships. But inevitably there are aspects of your life where you tense up to hide a truth from yourself, and that's something your inner circle can help you spot.

- **Swallow your pride.** There's a man who has worked around our house for more than fifteen years. He's walked our dog, cut our grass, and taken out our garbage. He's a true member of our family. I don't even know if he has a high school education, but I would talk to him about my most serious concerns sooner than I would talk to my lawyer—and I have a great lawyer. At times, he's said things that I didn't want to hear: *You've changed, Max. Money's going to your head. You're talking stupid.* Once some time ago he said, *Man, you sure got fat! What's going on with you?* I don't always enjoy his blatant honesty, but when I seek him out, I benefit from his ability to see changes in me that I can't see in myself.

- **Don't feel you have to take every suggestion.** Just because someone's in your inner circle doesn't mean that they're right all the time. My mother was a great source of wisdom for me about people in general, but not about my marriage. When she tried to tell me how to treat my wife, I said, Mom, I love you, but you were married four times; if you want to tell me what not to do, that's okay, but don't tell me how to do it right.

- **Change your idea of what makes a good conversation.** Will you always agree with the members of your inner circle? Of course not. With mine, I spend a lot of time discussing—and arguing. I want the people I'm closest with to challenge me, to martial their facts and make their case and see if they can get me to change my position. (I've heard this is President Obama's style as well.) It's not that I'm confrontational by nature, but if you feel strongly about something, I want you to show me that passion and give me the chance to be influenced by it. So with the members of my inner circle, the talk is spirited. I can think of a few colleagues who found it awkward the first time, but they discover that I never take any of it personally, even if we're talking about a subject that is personal. I know that their opinion, whether I like it or not, comes from a basis of respect and a willingness to disagree.

I keep emphasizing honesty and objectivity with your inner circle, both in what you should look for and what you should offer. Even so, honesty will only work if that frank talk comes in the service of wanting the other person to succeed and find satisfaction. For example, a former colleague of mine, now a close friend whom I consider a member of my inner circle, called to tell me about a new job offer she had received. The job sounded great, just what she had been waiting for, but it was going to mean moving across the country, and she was dating someone new she was excited about. She said, "I know we haven't been dating all that long, but I don't want to go anywhere unless he wants to go." I told her: you probably don't want to hear this right now, when you're newly in love, but you should make your career decisions based on your career goals, not your new guy. If the relationship matters that much, you'll feel it wherever you are and you'll respond to that feeling, but for now the relationship is new and untested, and this career opportunity is just the thing you've been waiting for. In other words, I told her straight, but I tried to tell her as respectfully as I could, acknowledging her feelings and talking in terms of what she had said to me in the past about where she wanted to be.

- **Take the bad with the good.** Any relationship, even—maybe especially—the most important ones, are going to have good times and bad times. You have to expect that. I always remind myself: no matter how you may feel on any given day, don't go into any conversation thinking, "How can I get out of this relationship? How would I cut it off?" Through the ups and downs, stay focused on whether it's more beneficial to be in a relationship than not—and with your inner circle, it almost always is.

- **Make sure those on your list feel your appreciation.** The heart of your inner circle is the mutual feeling that your best interests are shared. It only works when you respect and value the people close to you as much as you count on them to respect and value you. Although the people in your inner circle are probably the most likely people in the world to cut you slack when you need it, and to be patient when you're busy, it's up to you to be available for them just as they make themselves available for you.

EXPANDING YOUR INNER CIRCLE FROM PERSONAL TO PROFESSIONAL

SO FAR I'VE PUT the emphasis on how people with no special knowledge or qualifications can still be a source of great help and wisdom. I've stressed the value of trust. But as you progress in your career, you may find you need some people in your inner circle who understand the practical ins and outs of what you do, whether it's running a business, operating a machine, serving customers, or raising a family. How do you make sure you know when that day has come?

Don't confuse loyalty with skill.

I see it happen over and over, especially with professional athletes and artists. They surround themselves with an inner circle of dedicated people they can trust. In this they're usually a big step ahead of people from more conventional business backgrounds, who may find out too late that they have no one at work, maybe no one in the world, for whom they come first. But often, when that athlete's or artist's career takes off, they may imagine that their inner circle has business skills equal to their loyalty. They may give their trusted advisor more practical credit than they should, based on the feelings between them. At that point, it's time to ask what skills you can find among those in your inner circle, and what you need new members to provide.

Ask your existing inner circle to help add new members.

When you find that your inner circle needs to expand, don't push away the people who are already close. As you identify people with the professional expertise you need, you will have to make sure they are as trustworthy and as committed to your success as those already in your inner circle. When you have a few candidates in mind, let people already in your inner circle spend time with you and the new people you're considering. Even if they have no knowledge of the business issues, they may pick up on character, motives, and agenda.

In this way, the different members of your inner circle begin to create checks and balances. Over time, you will grow more comfortable going to different ones for different reasons, and they may each come to play very different roles. Some may never get as close personally but they know business or ideals. Frankly it's rare to find someone who can do it all. The goal is to give each person in your inner circle the chance to do the best for you that they can, as you do the best you can for them. Appreciate each one for how the two of you can get where you want to be.

Listen for the limits of people's skills.

When you are relying on people in your inner circle to handle things they are not qualified to do, there will be warning signs that you can hear; their lack of thorough knowledge, or their wrong fit with some aspect of your work, will lead them to say things that sound wrong. With my mother, for example, I came to realize that she would always speak authoritatively about whatever topic came up, whether she had the skill set to justify that confidence or not. If the question was medical, then she was a brain surgeon. If it was financial, she was a Wall Street financier. In our law office, where she was the office manager, she gave advice whenever she was asked, even to clients who thought she was one of the attorneys. But there were always moments in those conversations when she got out of her depth, and you could hear her straining to talk the way she thought an expert would talk. That was a small clue to what might have been a big problem if I hadn't caught it in time. Although I still respected her sense of people, I began to make sure, quietly, that our clients understood her role in the office.

I had a similar experience once with a leader and educator from my church. He wanted to get closer to me professionally, outside of the world of our church, and Jennifer and I decided to invite him to spend some time with the family so we could get to know each other better. We had a good time, but the conversation kept going off. Jennifer noticed it first. At some point in the conversation, the subject of her age came up. Our visitor, who happened to be white, started complimenting her: "You're so beautiful," he said, which was very flattering. "You're so lucky," which was fine, too. And then, "Black women just don't age!" That sounded strange to Jennifer, who, of course, ages like anyone else.

Then we were talking about my son Max's basketball game. He had been on fire that day, scored six buckets, and this man says, "He's the next Michael Jordan!" But we're from Indiana, Larry Bird fans, with no special feel for Michael Jordan—and really, my son isn't much like Michael Jordan at all. I suppose we were a little slow to smile. So he said, "But of course, he's such a smart kid. I mean, he's the next Barack Obama!"

It felt like this man, who as I say did a lot of good in the church, couldn't quite see us as anything but examples of our race. I believe he meant well, but we didn't feel the comfort, understanding, and respect that I would need to make him part of my inner circle. We realized the fit wasn't right because of the wrong notes in the conversation.

Change your idea of mentors.

There's no reason a mentor has to be older than you. The members of my inner circle are my mentors and my surrogate family; some are my peers and some are younger than I am. I've been mentored by someone in one area only to turn around and mentor that same person in a different area. Look for expertise, mutual goals, and a deep personal commitment to your success; nothing else matters.

HOW A BLACK MAN WITH A JEWISH NAME GOT TO NASCAR

I BEGAN THIS CHAPTER by saying that I would never have gotten where I am today, in a leadership position in the second biggest sport in America, if it hadn't been for my inner circle—and especially for Reggie White, the football great who became my client, my mentor, and my close friend. That story is the best illustration I know of the power of an inner circle to take you farther than you ever knew you could go.

I first met Reggie together with his wife, Sara. The Whites had met in church, and now they were interested in starting a gospel label. They heard about my work, and we had a meeting along with two NBA stars who, like Reggie, were also ministers. About fifteen minutes into that meeting, I knew that these people could not work together. While they shared some worthy goals, each of the three ballplayers had a different way he wanted to go about running the label, and all of them were strong-willed.

Still, I had a sense for what made them tick—the passion for the church and the drive of professional sports—and I could see where they wanted to be, so I went looking for someone who could help them rise above their disagreements and realize their goals. I spoke with a good friend of mine who was a manager at Warner Bros. Records. He liked their basic vision and he could see how their celebrity could get the new company the attention it would need. He also saw that while they lacked business expertise, he could provide the guidance for the day-to-day operation of the company. He was also interested in funding the company as an institutional investor.

I told Reggie that I thought that bringing in outside money and outside expertise was the only way to go, but he and the other ministers weren't comfortable with it. My friend at Warner Bros. was not African-American and not part of the church, and they didn't want to let an outsider dictate to them how to realize a religious vision. Reggie told me he would rather do it himself: spend his own cash and run it his way.

At that point, had I been willing to go along, I could have made some money. Instead, I told him the straight truth: I didn't think he could be successful with the gospel label. I said that I admired his vision but I didn't think he had the expertise to make it a practical success. It was a friendly conversation, showing respect on both sides, but it was a dead end. We could only agree to disagree. He went forward without me.

They launched the record label without me or my contact at Warner Bros., and soon Reggie had lost well into seven figures. Still, there were plenty of people benefitting from his willingness to spend his own money, and they kept Reggie and me apart for several months, not wanting me to stop the gravy train. Finally, I was called back to take a look at how the business was being run, and on my advice he shut it down.

I suppose at that point, from a conventional business perspective, we were done—he had taken his shot in the music business, I had helped him cut his losses, and the project was finished. But Reggie's prospects for founding a gospel label weren't all that mattered to me. I took an interest in him, his needs, and his larger situation. Reggie was not just one of the greatest defensive players football had ever seen; he had a larger vision. From early on, he spent his Sundays preaching on inner-city street corners. He gave generously to Christian charities and was known for only showing his amazing ferocity on the football field. He didn't fight and he didn't curse; he treated everyone with respect. As he told *Sports Illustrated*, "I believe that I've been blessed with physical ability in order to gain a platform to preach the gospel. . . . I try to live a certain way, and maybe that'll have some kind of effect. I think God has allowed me to have an impact on a few people's lives." It was this combination of his greatness as a player and his religious commitments that led to the nickname that stuck with him: the Minister of Defense.

From the day I met him, I wanted to get to know him as a person and not just how we might do business together. When we talked, we talked about our lives, our families, our dreams, and our aspirations. We talked about our passion for sports and our hope to see people of color succeed. We talked about wanting to live up to our values, which in Reggie's case would lead him and Sara to build Hope Place—a shelter for unwed mothers near their home in rural Tennessee—and the Alpha & Omega Ministry, which sponsored a community development bank in Knoxville. Even while we were disagreeing about his scheme for his gospel label, and later when we shut it down, our conversations kept deepening. Our relationship grew stronger. I knew there might be potential for other business opportunities with Reggie, but the most important thing for me was to be true to him and to Sara.

One day I told him that Jennifer and I had gotten engaged to be married; Reggie insisted he would perform the ceremony. Although Jennifer and I had already set a date, the Packers could only give him a very limited choice of days off, so we changed our wedding day so he could officiate.

At a certain point after we shut down the gospel label, he told me that he wanted to make some changes in the way he handled his career and his public life. He said that I combined business skill, honesty, integrity, and a desire to help people of color grow, and for those reasons he wanted me to become his agent. I had become a part of his inner circle; now he was looking to expand his inner circle to promote his professional growth, and he wanted to include me there, too, in a formal role. (By contractual agreement, his current agent had to remain his official agent-of-record for life; technically, I became his co-agent.)

Even after I started working for him, we didn't just talk about his career. We talked about everything, from business to marriage, from spirituality to family. One day, he called me up with a big idea I didn't expect. He was always very proud of his daughter's singing voice, he reminded me, and he wanted to help with her career. Now he told me he was going to make a record of his daughter singing while he played the harp. He had already called someone in the music business to find out which harp to buy, and he was taking lessons over the phone. Would I help him make the record? Did I think we would have a hit? I told him, "That sounds great, Reggie, but you've got to kill the harp. No one's going to buy defensive lineman Reggie White playing the harp." I would be lying if I said his feelings weren't hurt at first, but he took it like a champ.

How does this story lead to me getting hired to run the best-known team in NASCAR? It doesn't. The harp album was a complete dead end, and that's the point. Reggie and I shared our ideas and dreams, big and small, smart and dumb. We stepped in when we thought the other was going to do something foolish and we worked together when we had an idea we both thought was good. That's what it means to be part of someone's inner circle. You're in for life, you give your honest best, and you're open to talk about anything.

The more we talked about racing, the more we felt that the way to make a difference in the sport was to launch a minority-owned team. It seemed the best place to be was in the bush league competition, like the minor leagues. One day on the phone Reggie suggested we meet to get started on our ideas for getting into NASCAR. I told him that I would love to meet, but not on the day he was available. My son had a tricycle race that day. The kids were going to meet in the schoolyard for their own Indy 500 and I had promised to be there to watch.

Suddenly Reggie wasn't talking business. He was all excited about my son's race. He announced that he was going to fly up for it, and sure enough when the day came, there he was, the great Reggie White, recently named to the NFL Hall of Fame's All-Time Team, hanging with my little boy at his school like it was no big deal—like it was, for that moment, the most important thing in the world to him. Thinking of it today still brings tears to my eyes. Reggie understood how important it was for me to show up for my kids' events, because my own parents were so rarely able to show up for me. Seeing Reggie do the same made me feel once again that I would do anything for him. That tells you more than anything why I was in Reggie's inner circle.

After the kids were done racing, we talked about what we could do to convince the top people in NASCAR. We shared our best ideas freely, and we were free in our criticism when one of us had a "harp" idea. We were doing business but we were talking like brothers. And in the presentations we gave, I think our commitment and our vision, refined by this generous listening and talking, came through. We combined Reggie's incomparable competitive experience and celebrity with my vision that in the twenty-first century, when the costs of running a sports team are so high, the owners must understand that they are in the entertainment business, because only succeeding in that business will cover the costs of a winning team. A lot of people have come around to that way of seeing now, but at the time it was something new, and I think that together we were able to convey the excitement and the promise of what we could do for this sport we both loved.

Sadly, Reggie passed away before these plans could bear fruit. He suffered a heart attack when he was only forty-three years old. But I continued to pursue our vision, drawing on the connections we had made, the ideas we developed, and the goodwill we spread together, and while NASCAR doesn't yet have a minority-owned top-tier team, it has had its first minority president at the cup level. I said earlier that the power of an inner circle is that it's stronger than any individual project or goal, and in this case the inspiration, the focus, the planning, and the commitment nurtured between Reggie and me outlived him. I owe my success to the dedication of my inner circle, Reggie foremost among them.

• • • • • CHAPTER SEVEN • • • • •

Find Your **Ambassadors**

THERE HAVE BEEN DAYS when I've doubted whether my rules could get me where I needed to go. Not because the principles I've described aren't effective, but because it can seem that following them is too much to do. I can't be everywhere at once—even with the best technology ever devised. I can't talk to everyone every day. I can't learn every language or force people to listen to me when their minds are closed. Over time, I've noticed that those moments of doubt are strongest not when I've had setbacks, but when I've had big successes. A new opportunity opens up for me, or I'm blessed with the chance to conduct my business on a much larger stage, and the question arises again: will these simple rules still get me where I need to go?

If you think that motivating people by knowing what makes them tick means extra work for you, you're right—but don't worry. You don't have to do it alone. As soon as you start helping others to be heard and be taken care of, you have the chance to make them your ambassadors. They will carry your messages, solve your problems, take care of those who rely on you, and guarantee your success in ways you could never do on your own. What starts out seeming like extra work winds up making your life easier.

I remember when I became president of DEI and I met my four hundred employees for the first time. Of course, I couldn't "meet" them all, not in a personal sense, but Teresa Earnhardt, the owner of the company and my new boss, held an event so that everyone could raise a glass of champagne and welcome me. She wanted me to introduce myself to the company and make clear why I was there and what I wanted to accomplish.

Five minutes before it was to begin, some of Teresa's people came to me, saying, "Do you know how important this is? These people are going to rely on every word you say. And you know, a year from now, they'll remember any promise you make. Are you ready?" I thought to myself, oh, my.

The kind of nervousness I felt at that moment was familiar, and it went back a long way. It reminded me of being the new kid at school (as I had been so many times), the new guy at work, or the new boyfriend meeting the family. This time, there were hundreds of people I had to connect with, reassure, and inform, but just as in all those past situations, I was facing a big room filled mostly with strangers and there was no way I could take my usual approach. I couldn't chat with each of them one at a time, to put them at ease and draw them out about what made them tick. Had I outgrown my rules? I definitely felt like the outsider, and at that moment being an outsider felt nothing like an advantage.

At the same time, I knew Teresa's people were right. This was my chance to make a good first impression, and it mattered. There was a lot of work to be done at the company, starting with a huge problem of morale. The workers didn't know who was in charge; they hardly seemed to expect good leadership anymore. Where there should have been open communication and a clear chain of command, there was chaos and confusion. I was supposed to be the guy who would change all of that, but for now I was just the unfamiliar face who had to convince hundreds of people that I belonged at the head of their company.

What did I do? First, I thought about those four hundred people and what their goals and feelings might be as they listened to my speech. I put aside my concerns and thought about theirs. What was important to them? It seemed to me it came down to two ideas:

1. Most of these people were here because of Dale Senior's legacy. During his life as a driver and as owner of the team to which he gave his name, he had accomplished more than anyone in the history of the sport, winning seventy-six races and seven championships. He left behind a tradition that still spoke to the fans. The people I was about to meet were dedicated to Dale, accustomed to winning, and concerned about the direction of the company.

2. Most of these people were suspicious of me, and understandably so. They were concerned that I wasn't like them—probably even more than the fact that I was African-American, they were concerned that I came from outside of racing.

When the time came for my speech, I tried to be as honest and as emotionally transparent as I could be. I told them that it was intimidating being up there in front of all of them, and that so far, since I had arrived in Charlotte, everything was going horribly. I told them I had promised my wife that when I came to DEI, I would have a less stressful job than at Sony/BMG, but that already there was more stress. I told them how I had promised her she would be glad to get away from the snow in Indianapolis, but the first day we got down to Charlotte, it snowed. I said I knew I had my work cut out for me.

Then I talked a little about who I was and what values I brought to my new job. I acknowledged that I didn't come from racing and implied that as an African-American I was different, but I stressed the core values I believed we all shared: a strong work ethic, an appreciation for people, and a belief that as president it was my job to do everything I possibly could to support them.

Most of all, I told them that no matter who we all were, the common legacy of Dale Senior bound us together like a family. We were all there together to honor him. When Dale had raced, he had mainly worn the number three, and that inspired me to offer a new mission statement based on three goals:

- To win: on the track, in business, at the office, and in our personal lives.
- To serve: the fans, each other, and our commercial partners.
- To grow the business and spread love of the sport.

When I had explained this new mission statement, I asked them all to come up and sign a written copy, as a symbol of the goals we shared. That gave everyone a reason to come up to the front of the room, if they felt like it. As they did, I watched to see what would happen, looking for nonverbal signs of how I was doing. In other words, even as president of the company, and even as I faced hundreds of strangers, I was making use of the same approach I described in chapter 1, to get below the superficial niceties and begin to connect with people in terms of what makes them tick.

How did it go? As employees came up to sign the mission statement, some stopped to talk to me. Some had done a little research on me, as I could hear in their remarks. A few said things like, "Hey, Max, I listen to Kirk Franklin" (or another Zomba artist), as if to show that whatever our differences, we could connect through the music. Some found things in common with my hometown ("My grandmother lived in Indianapolis") and that sort of thing. I wasn't all that concerned with the particulars of what they said; what mattered to me lay underneath the words. I was listening to understand whether they were open to connecting with me or trying to keep their distance. I found that there were more people trying to find ways we could connect than those trying to show me how we were different. That was how I measured the success of my speech, as a start toward finding what we had in common and how we could work together.

But it was just a start. I came home that night reminded that my one-on-one techniques could never be enough to succeed with a big group. I didn't have the time to do it all myself, no more than singers can perform live for everyone who might want to buy their albums;

no more than politicians can shake hands with everyone whose vote they need to win. I needed to find some ambassadors.

AMBASSADORS GET YOU HEARD

AN AMBASSADOR IS ANYONE who bestows good will from one group to another group, making it possible to establish relationships so you can all work together. Some ambassadors move between countries. Others go from management to the shop floor. I needed ambassadors to go between me and my new employees. I also needed ambassadors who could talk for me to the greater community.

Ambassadors may be members of your inner circle or strangers you've only met today. They may have formal leadership positions or they may only be social leaders. The president of a company or a country is a natural ambassador, but so is the receptionist who talks to everyone coming in and out of the door, or the person who pushes the donut cart through the halls, making conversation along the way. The power of ambassadors comes not from their formal titles but from the personal credibility they have in their group, a credibility that lets them influence their group to welcome an outsider or to close him out.

When do you need an ambassador? Whenever the people you need to partner with for success can't hear you. Sometimes, as in my example, there are too many people to reach one-on-one. Sometimes the people you need to connect with might be too afraid, angry, or uninformed to give you a chance, which means they won't be listening to you no matter how much you talk. Sometimes they are willing to listen but you don't speak their language, either literally or because of some gap in your background that makes it hard for you to grasp what matters to them. The bigger the opportunity, the more likely that you can't succeed without the right ambassadors.

When I gave my introductory speech at Dale Earnhardt Inc., I knew that what I said didn't matter as much as what the influencers and the tastemakers in the company and beyond were going to say about it afterward. Even more than at some other companies where I had worked, I knew that being president didn't actually give me much credibility—it might even have hurt me. As I've said, by the time I arrived, our people didn't even expect management to lead. It had been a long time since the team had won a race, and few seemed to believe that management could help them do that. To change that perception, I went looking for an ambassador to inspire trust and confidence, a natural leader with a real understanding of excellence in racing who could help me restore trust in management. But where to begin? I was brand new there myself.

I've already described part of the way I tried to put my fellow workers at ease and learn what mattered to them. I traveled from race to race not on the owner's jet, but with the team. Every day when I went to the track, I wore the team competition uniform, so everyone would see that I wasn't just the new "suit." I was part of the team. I spent a lot of down time with our employees, eating, drinking, and talking in the back of our haulers or in the motor coach lot, so I could hear their concerns and their perspective on what was really going on with the company. Just by being there, I was letting them know that while I might have a different background and a different job title, I didn't think I was any different or greater than they were. I was showing them that I wanted to help them do their jobs better. So far, though, the only ambassador was me. I was the one doing all the work of listening and spreading the word about how we could improve the company.

The people who really knew what made the company tick kept mentioning one name, Rex Garrett. I kept hearing that he ran "the best gear shop in the sport." Now, most people don't even know that the gear shop is where they work on the drive train, and that the drive train, arguably, is the most important component of a competitive racing vehicle besides the motor. The gear shop just isn't a sexy area of the sport. But Rex Garrett had been with the company for eleven years, doing this unsexy and crucial work, and those who worked with him had noticed. Again and again, I heard that he was focused, organized, dedicated, loyal, smart, and an incredibly hard worker. He had tremendous credibility in the company. Here, I thought, was a potential ambassador.

When I met him, I confirmed all that I had heard, and I learned something else about him: he was about to quit. He wanted to make a bigger impact on the company than his job allowed, he wasn't getting the chance, and he was just about sick of it. But instead of letting him give notice, I elevated him to director of Motor Sports Operations. Now he would oversee manufacturing for the entire race staff. He had a platform from which to put his ideas into practice, and he sprang into action. Rex had ideas about how processes could be reorganized and made more efficient, and he found ways to cut costs. He identified co-workers whose opinions were not being taken seriously enough in the company and others who could perform at a higher level.

As he got to work, the benefits came fast and they were amazing— for the company, for him, and for me. Pride in the company shot up because I hadn't brought in someone from outside: one of their own guys had worked hard and gotten recognized. Respect for me shot up as well, because everyone saw I knew enough to trust in others when they had more experience than I did with the daily workings of competitive racing. Rex was inspired to work twice as hard as before, doing an amazing job identifying and addressing issues all over the company. And once he was in this new position, as he appreciated that he and I were trying to reach the same overall goals, he started to make it his business to explain that to people. All over the company, he told people, "You have no idea how many problems Max is working on. You have to see what a tremendous job Max is doing." A couple of sentences like that from a co-worker they respected did more for me with my employees than a dozen speeches and a hauler full of champagne. There was literally nothing I could have said or done that would have been as effective for me as what he said on my behalf. He had become my ambassador.

THE FIRST LEVEL: CREDIBILITY

THERE ARE A FEW levels to the work an ambassador can do for you. The first and most important is also the simplest. You need an ambassador to connect with people you can't connect with yourself, to validate your credibility. To help you on that first level, ambassadors don't have to share your whole vision or understand all your plans. They just have to clear the path for you, removing the obstacles that keep people from giving you a chance. Often it's as simple as someone saying, "Have you met Jane yet? She's all right. You ought to hear what she's got to say." But far more important than any particular words an ambassador says or doesn't say, at this early stage, is how they use their own credibility and authority to change the way others see you and hear you. Like the music in a church service—or, to take a very different setting, like music in the background at a party or on a date— what the ambassador says changes the mood in which people listen, helping them hear you better and guiding their response to what you say and do.

How do you find an ambassador? To begin, look for people who have the influence in their community to open people's minds. It can be the shop foreman or the gossip at the water cooler—anyone who gets attention, anyone who gets heard. The writer of the newsletter. The person who keeps a jar of candy on her desk so everyone will stop by to chat. What you need from them was summed up in that old shampoo commercial, where two people try out the shampoo, and they tell two friends, who each tell two friends, who each tell two friends, until word has spread exponentially. Because what mattered to me was not just that Rex Garrett talked to people on my behalf, but that he got conversations going that started other people talking: "Did you hear what Rex said about Max Siegel?" He wasn't just giving me compliments. He single-handedly launched a finely tooled word-of-mouth marketing campaign.

The idea that ambassadors can create a domino effect on behalf of your credibility is both cutting edge and very old school. The cutting edge term is "viral marketing," something I've used with success in both the music business and racing. Viral marketing relies on people with "high social networking potential"—that is, ambassadors—to pass along messages that then spread on their own from person to person like a virus. With the advent of the Internet and cell phones, there are all kinds of high-tech viral marketing campaigns: people share video clips, images, games, text messages, and so on with their friends and the people in their personal or professional social networks, and these viral messages about a particular brand or product carry extra weight and credibility based on who sent them to you.

As much as I appreciate these high-tech forms as an aid to my business, I also like to remember that these new methods are just ways to reproduce with technology what has always happened when an ambassador gets out a message. When Jesus gathered his disciples, and they went out as his ambassadors to spread the word to others who spread the word even further, that was viral marketing, old school.

So whether you're using the latest social networking site or old-fashioned conversation, there will always be an opportunity to influence people in this way, because people will always have a need to know about the new people and ideas that appear in their lives. Most people don't want to do that work themselves. They don't want to gather all the facts and analyze the character of every new person who comes in the door, or every opportunity that comes their way. Instead, they rely on those they trust or admire, because it saves them time, adds to their understanding, and keeps them in harmony with their group.

I even see it happening spontaneously with my kids. The oldest will tell one of the younger ones: you had better listen up now or you're going to be in trouble—and sometimes his message gets through better than the same words from mom or dad. Or if one of the kids is afraid, another may say, "It's okay, it's going to be all right," just as Jennifer and I might do—but when they get there first, they can often deliver the message more effectively. I've noticed that they do this without anyone asking them to; it's a natural part of the family communication. People will always have that need for help in understanding events around them and making decisions, so there will always be an opportunity for effective ambassadors to spread their messages.

INFLUENCE FOLLOWS ATTENTION

HOW DO YOU IDENTIFY the people who can do that for you? Locating people with influence doesn't require any special gift or sophisticated technique. Whatever environment you're working in, you need to spend time with the people you want to work with, listening and watching until you can follow the flow of attention. Don't be distracted by behavior—just because someone acts self-important or talks a lot doesn't mean they have a lot of influence. Look instead for the person to whom attention is paid. Whom does everybody talk to? Whom does everybody talk about? The person who gets attention in a group can influence that group.

1. Listen for the names people mention the most. Often you'll notice, as I did with Rex, a name that gets mentioned a lot. Some people will refer to them in stories. "Last week, Rex had a problem like that." Other people will defer to them. "Oh, I would have to check with so-and-so about that." "You might want to ask so-and-so." The repetition of their name is your clue.

2. Look for the peer leader, not the person formally in

charge. In sports teams or other groups organized as teams and under the leadership of a coach, often the coach is not the influencer. Instead, the coach will identify the influential person and make him or her captain. The natural leader given a special place among peers will be the one the others follow.

3. In a social setting, look for the trendsetters. Whom do people want to talk about, good or bad? Whom do they want to emulate or be seen with? Earlier in this book, I told the story of my cousin's crew, the group of troublemakers whose acceptance I needed before I could accomplish anything else in high school. My cousin was that trendsetter: the guys dressed like him, the girls wanted to be seen with him, and when he said I was okay even if I wasn't staying out all night, I was okay.

4. In a hierarchy, learn who the leaders want to please. The formal leadership of an organization always has a feel for where the influence lies, and it's not necessarily with them. When you meet with the official leaders, listen for whom they are impressed by, whom they admire, and whom they want to keep satisfied. When I'm getting to know church leaders, I listen for remarks like, "You need to go talk to so-and-so; he's been here for forty years." Or, "Better watch out for Sister Mary. . . ."

5. Value troublemakers. Just because someone gets negative attention doesn't mean they aren't influential. Attention is powerful whether it's positive, negative, or mixed. One disgruntled person may be expressing the frustrations of the entire group. When I first met Rex Garrett, he felt that the company had overlooked him, and I gathered that he had some choice words to say about management. I didn't take offense; I sensed an opportunity. Often it's the troublemaker or the hell-raiser whose approval can start to turn things around.

WHY SHOULD AN AMBASSADOR WANT TO HELP YOU?

ONCE YOU'VE IDENTIFIED POTENTIAL ambassadors by the influence they can have in their realm, you need to motivate them to work with you. I've noticed that for some people I've tried to mentor, this step feels mysterious and difficult. It's as if they can't come up with any reason that others would want to speak up on their behalf. Doing your own part, on the job or in the community, is one thing, they tell me; but this ambassador business—isn't that something different?

My answer is, no, it's more of the same. When you hope someone will become your ambassador, even in a very limited way, you're proposing a kind of partnership. In every partnership, our rules apply. To move someone to work with you, you have to offer them the possibility of mutual benefit. Rex Garrett had dreams and goals of what he could accomplish at work if someone would give him the chance, and I gave him that chance. There was benefit to him in being my ambassador, and that's why it worked.

Of course, I was president of the company, so I was in the position to give Rex Garrett a promotion. But I don't mean to suggest that your ambassadors will necessarily work for you, or that you have to offer them something that very few people can offer. That idea would only reinforce the wrong impression some people have, that gathering and inspiring ambassadors requires you to offer some special compensation. So is there a secret to influence after all?

I suppose the secret is that influence is a lot less complicated than some people make it out to be. Most of us on the planet, including almost everyone you would ever hope to have as your ambassador, have the same basic desire. What most people want is to feel that someone understands and appreciates what they go through in their lives. In other words, we're all waiting for someone else to notice us, acknowledge us, and help us out with the things that make us tick. So if you're looking for a secret to motivating your ambassadors, you might try an old Biblical principle: *do unto others as you would have them do to you.*

Notice that it's not just a negative principle—it's not just *don't do what you don't want done,* don't kill, don't lie, don't steal, and so forth. It's positive: *do.* Do give others the attention, the sympathy, the help and advice, the trust and the loyalty you wish someone would give you. Do it whenever you can. Of course, I'm not perfect. I have my own motivations and shortcomings, but this is the ideal I try to live. It is the heart of my approach to leadership, which is to lead by serving. If I am conducting a performance review for one of my employees, I try to imagine what would be best—most comfortable, most informative, most useful—for me if my performance was under review, and to offer that to my employee. I am the leader, but I lead by serving the employee's needs.

As a result, when I identify someone as an influencer who might benefit me as an ambassador, I begin immediately to get to know what makes him or her tick, so I can discover what benefits I can offer.

1. If the person is puzzling over a question, whether it's where to eat lunch or in what direction to take his or her career, I listen and I take it seriously. If I have an insight, I offer it freely.
2. If the person lacks for something and I can be useful in getting it, even in a small way, I try to do it for them as a favor.
3. If the person has a longer-term goal and I can help them toward it in some reasonable way, I do. I share information, contacts, and experience; I'm open to investing in new ventures. As Tom Silverman of Tommy Boy Records always told me, there are two ways to view the world, as a place of scarcity or a place of abundance. I try to respond to people's needs out of a sense of abundance. I give away a lot for free.

There is a kind of magic in this approach, and it's not that you get a reward for handing out favors. What makes the difference is that when you offer someone help, freely, you show that person that you are not just out for yourself; you are committed to finding some mutual benefit together. So once again we come back to basics: you are helping them to achieve whatever it is that makes them tick. There is nothing more likely to inspire others to become your ambassadors.

I've seen this approach work in every business I know. It was crucial to me when I was just starting out. When I first started work at a law firm, I ran into a wall. I wanted to focus on sports law, but I quickly learned that almost no one in the firm considered that a viable route for a young attorney. It was a typical dilemma for a new hire in any kind of business: the company might have brought me in partly because of my fresh ideas, but once I arrived I clashed with the organization's accepted ways. In this case, most of the senior attorneys didn't even recognize sports law as a legitimate legal specialty—they just viewed it as an excuse to run off to games and hang out with players. The underlying problem was that billing in sports law was different than in other practice areas. Most of our firm's business was conducted on the traditional model of billing a client for each hour you worked. But in sports and entertainment, lawyers are paid not by the hour but as a percentage of each deal they close with a player or an artist. As a result, you may work for weeks or months with someone before you can bill them for anything—and to someone unfamiliar with that approach, it may look as if you're not working at all, because you're not filling in your billable hours on your time sheet every week.

I was under a lot of pressure from senior attorneys to change my focus when I found an ambassador. Jack Swarbrick had a long-standing reputation at the firm as a smart, effective, and well-respected lawyer. I discovered that we shared a passion for sports, and that while he had begun his practice doing intellectual property work and billing hours the traditional way, over the years he had expanded into a general sports practice that the firm had come to accept. Jack was glad to find a young attorney like me, who was interested in his specialty and eager to learn how he had made a success of it, and he became my ambassador, acting as my supervisor, my cover with the other senior partners, my manager, and my public relations representative all at once. In time, he introduced me to the mayor and the governor. He helped me make connections that led to my being appointed to the city Arts Council and the Parks and Recreation Board, helping to get my name out and to make connections that could further my success. And everywhere I went, I told people how he was guiding me and shaping my development as an attorney.

But our relationship went beyond the familiar one of mentor and protégé: just as he had become my ambassador, in time I became his. Jack was an extremely accomplished lawyer, but he was not a self-promoter; he didn't seem to appreciate how much people valued his opinion, not just on legal matters but on business ones as well. As I gained his trust, I encouraged him to offer his services more widely, so he could have an impact not just as a lawyer but on the greater community landscape, whether in sports, business, or industry. He began to be offered positions on corporate boards, not just as legal counsel but as chair. He was instrumental in the campaign to move the NCAA headquarters from Kansas to Indianapolis, bringing jobs and prestige to the city. He did the same for most of the national governing bodies of Olympic sports. He became known as a gatekeeper and pillar of the amateur athletic community, both collegiate and Olympic. Then in 2008, when the University of Notre Dame was looking for a new athletic director to run what many consider to be the premier collegiate athletic program in the country, they found what they were looking for in Jack Swarbrick. The same techniques for finding one's ambassadors that had gotten me established as a newcomer to the company had led him to his dream job, the crowning accomplishment of his career.

THEY DON'T ALWAYS COME
ACCORDING TO PLAN

YOU WON'T ALWAYS FIND your ambassadors by making a conscious plan and taking intentional steps to meet and connect with them. Like opportunities in general, the best ambassadors may turn out to be the ones you wouldn't anticipate, didn't seek, and couldn't arrange. Sometimes they might even work for the competition or play on the other team. Two of my most important ambassadors in NASCAR, for example, have been Dale Earnhardt Jr. and his sister, Kelley Earnhardt-Elledge. (To fans and to the general public, Junior, the star driver, is the name that's well known. But Kelley is his agent, his business manager, and the general manager of his organization. To team owners, administrators, and sponsors in the sport, she is the heart of his business.) As important as they have been in establishing my credibility, I never sought them out as ambassadors.

As I described in chapter 1, we met as adversaries in a very tense negotiation. That difficult negotiation, however, didn't stop me from taking an interest in them and trying to learn what made them tick. I tried to understand what would be best for Junior and Kelley and to offer them help achieving it. Both before and after Junior made his decision to leave DEI and race with another team, I told him: "Look, everyone is selling you on where you ought to be. But at some point you have to do what makes you happy and not try to please your fans or me or even your sister." I backed up my personal advice by being as helpful as I could. Sometimes there were relatively small things he needed to get done at DEI to move his career forward, such as getting approval from the company to endorse a new sponsor. Relations between the two siblings and the rest of management had grown tense, but I would do what I could to ease the tension and get approval for actions that would be mutually beneficial for all of us, such as a product endorsement that was stalled. Sometimes when Kelley had a strong plan in mind and Junior wasn't convinced, I could be the outside voice saying to Junior: yes, that seems like a wise business move. Sometimes Kelley and I talked about her own career path and how she could continue to grow as a professional herself.

Soon, some very interesting things began to happen. Kelley and I were seen chatting together in front of each other's haulers, getting along just fine in the middle of the controversy. Our collegial relationship made a statement that was picked up by the media: I wasn't making a choice between the two Earnhardt siblings and Teresa, who was their stepmother and my boss. At the time, there was a tendency for some journalists and fans to treat Junior's departure like a divorce and take sides, but Junior and Kelley were giving me the chance to show the fans a more positive approach.

The more I was able to have a positive impact on Junior, the more he felt inspired to tell people about me. Increasingly, both of them were asked, "What's Max like?" Kelley spread a lot of goodwill for me on the business side of the sport and Junior spoke to the other drivers and crew members and to the press. From his first interview after he met me, through the conflict over whether Junior or DEI would keep the rights to drive the number eight car, he kept telling people that I was working as hard as I could to solve problems. And after DEI merged with Chip Ganassi Racing, and I left to take over NASCAR's Drive for Diversity program, he told the *New England Racing News:* "He may be pulling the wool over my eyes, but I like him. He is a really good guy in my opinion. I hope that he's involved in the sport for quite some time." Just as nothing I could have accomplished within my company could have done me a fraction of the good that came from the opinion of an ambassador like Rex Garrett, nothing I could have said to the press could compare to the benefits of having Junior and Kelley as my ambassadors.

That Junior and Kelley played that role for me came as a surprise to some people in racing, and at first, to be honest, I was one of them. But while I didn't see it coming, I recognized that this is the sort of result you get when you stick to your "rules." That experience reaffirmed for me that when it comes to motivating other people to be your ambassadors, your focus shouldn't be on manipulating the behavior of the people with the power to spread goodwill for you, but on making sure that your behavior toward them remains consistent with the goodwill you want to generate.

WHO HAS TIME FOR ALL OF THIS?

YOU MIGHT BE WONDERING: doesn't this approach take a lot of time? Am I suggesting that you have to talk to everyone you know every day, listening to understand, appreciating them, and so on? Some people imagine I must spend my days (and nights) in nonstop conversation. But who has time for that?

The answer is, no, I don't. I try to treat everybody I meet the same way, pleasant and friendly, but I don't waste a lot of time. I talk to very few people a lot, and I don't expect you to spend all your time talking, either. The key is to be sensitive to the ways in which each relationship has its natural rhythm.

When I had my first meeting with Junior and Kelley, it was one short meeting, but I could feel the potential for a relationship to grow, and I made a point of following up with them. There was a period when we were in contact very frequently. But once you have given a relationship its foundation, it's not necessary to be in contact frequently. With my best friend and former partner, Mickey Carter, for example, I may go three months or more between conversations, but still I get more from talking with him once in three months than from some people I talk to casually every day.

To manage my time while still connecting with people in the ways that matter so much, I do three things.

1. I conduct myself according to my rules with everyone I meet. It's simplest that way because it's consistent, it's true to what I believe, and the result is that every conversation is a chance to learn what makes people tick and how we might work together, including whether they might be an ambassador for me—or whether I might be one for them.

2. I stay alert for those moments when the other person does open up to me, and we discover how we could benefit each other.

3. I remain aware of the natural changes in every relationship. If we're working on something together or just enjoying each other's company, then it's time to spend more time together. If our project is done or we've had some good times, then it's time to move on for a while. We'll keep in touch, but lightly. I'll make sure you know I'm there for you if you need me, but we don't have to talk a lot to prove it.

HIGHER-LEVEL AMBASSADORS

SO FAR I'VE FOCUSED on how ambassadors can provide you with the basic acceptance and credibility you need to start the conversations and the relationships that will move you toward your goals. Beyond validating your credibility, though, there are two further levels at which your ambassadors can be crucial to your success: they can promote your agenda and they can share the burden of leadership.

Ambassadors can translate and promote your agenda.

I want to make clear that an ambassador provides more than a reference. He or she is not just someone who will say on your behalf: "Oh yes, so-and-so worked for me or with me, and he or she was productive and reliable, a great worker, etc." Or: "Sure, so-and-so is a good guy. He was in my car pool/church choir/poker game." Of course, it's helpful to be able to provide references when you are trying to establish a new role, whether at work or in social situations, but a reference is essentially a passive summary: a reference confirms facts about what you have done in the past. By contrast, an ambassador promotes your agenda now, going out of his or her way to influence people's opinions and to build consensus to support you. They don't just confirm facts about your past; they help others to imagine that you could help them build a successful future.

My first important ambassador in this sense was my sister Traci, back when I wanted to start an agency representing sports and entertainment figures. I had no connections in the industry when I was starting out. My first idea about how to get my foot in the door of the music business was to use my father's old connections. So I started to call people my dad had known. I even offered to work for free in the industry to get experience. What happened? No one was interested. I'm not sure anyone even called me back. I was nobody yet in the industry, and I was treated as a nobody.

My sister, meanwhile, had established herself in radio. She was general manager of a station in Charlotte. As I described in chapter 2, she was the one who suggested I meet John P. Kee, because he was having such success with his music and his ministry that he needed representation. I've described how I went down to meet him and how we bonded by playing basketball, but the fact is that even connecting with him in that personal way might not have closed the deal for my partner and me.

When Mickey and I drove down to meet him, John P. Kee was already very hot, with lots of people offering to represent him, including lawyers and managers well known in the gospel world. He had long-standing relationships in Charlotte, while Mickey and I were just visitors from out of town. We all had a great personal connection from the start, but these other factors weighed against us.

That's where Traci was so important as my ambassador. She knew John personally, so she had his trust. She was accepted within the Christian music community, so she could vouch for me in the terms that were most important to John as a minister. Just as I would later go between my secular boss at Zomba and our Christian artists, translating their needs into terms the other side could understand, she translated me into John's terms. Finally, she was a success in the music business, with experience programming Christian music on her radio station, so she could make the case that I understood the business side as well. At that early stage, I wasn't the one who best understood John's deep motivations and how to help him imagine the success he could have with Mickey and me. Traci did that for me.

Once I began representing John, he then became my own biggest ambassador. People would call him from all over the gospel world and beyond, saying, "Tell me about Max. What kind of work does he do? Is he cool? Does he respect your vision?" Both Tony Gwynn and Reggie White, when they were getting to know me, contacted him as a respected minister with strong Christian values who could give them an assessment of me, even though they were in sports and he was in music. But John didn't just give me a good reference; he vouched for me and promoted me, saying, "You ought to get together with Max. You will be so glad that you did."

Ambassadors share in the burdens of leadership.

At the highest level, an ambassador goes beyond preparing people to listen to you, or even promoting your worth or translating your words, and begins to speak for you, almost in your name. This happened to me with a very gifted assistant, Ayana Rivera, who worked with me for many years. As we continued to work together, she came to understand both my vision and my style, and often she could answer questions that people had for me as well as I would have answered them myself. Most people felt that if they talked to her, they talked to me, which saved me an enormous amount of time. I came to rely on her not just to prepare the way for me, but to act as a leader herself, almost as my second in command.

The most important ambassadors you can have are those people who can speak for you, expanding your range by influencing people you don't have the ability or the time to reach yourself. Finding your ambassadors, in other words, is the beginning of gathering your leadership team. When you look at effective leaders anywhere, whether in business, politics, church, or family, you find that they surround themselves with co-leaders whose qualifications go beyond their job skills. What makes a team effective is that in addition to competence, they share a common vision, a similar style, and an ability to deliver a consistent message.

A TEAM OF SERVANT-LEADERS

THE APPROACH I'M DESCRIBING in this book, based on knowing what makes people tick, is at heart an approach to leadership. You may already recognize yourself as a leader or you may find this idea surprising, but from the moment you first try to see where someone else wants to be and how you can get there together, you are both a servant, helping the other person toward what he wants, and a leader, showing the way. It doesn't matter what your job title may be or if you have no title at all. You might be the head of your corporate team or a new hire, but you're a leader as soon as you imagine a vision of mutual benefit, and as soon as you assist others to help you realize a vision.

How do you recruit these high-level ambassadors? You shouldn't have to recruit them at all. Don't go interviewing strangers for the role. If you have been following the approach in this chapter and in this book, you will already be drawing people to you, some of whom will already be your ambassadors in lower-level ways, vouching for your credibility and translating your approach for others. Listen for the ones who understand not just that you have some worthy goals, and not just what you have said in the past, but what you are likely to say in related situations in the future. Look for the ones who can understand the agenda behind your actions, and those who take it upon themselves to work for your larger goals in ways you haven't even requested. That is, look for the ones who show themselves to be servant-leaders. They are presenting themselves to you; it's up to you to recognize and select them. Sometimes you'll do this formally, by offering them a position or promotion in your organization or group. In other situations, the selection is more informal, as it was when Junior and Kelley began inviting me to socialize with them. Either way, it's a clear chance to deepen the relationship and shoulder some of your burdens together.

I've written a lot already in this book about motivating ambassadors at the lower levels, to speak for your credibility and to promote you and your goals. But how do you motivate at the higher levels? Are there special techniques of leadership that only come into play once you are gathering a whole team of ambassadors to serve as your co-leaders? There are not. One of the biggest mistakes I see successful people make is to toss aside the principles and approaches that built their success because of a confused idea that now they have outgrown the old rules. All the old rules still apply; the question is how to apply them on a bigger stage, with more actors and more at stake.

Motivating ambassadors to share the burdens of leadership is not any different from moving anyone else to do anything. You have to make clear the mutual benefit. And the most powerful benefit you can offer is you. The ambassadors who will work hardest, feel most loyal, and get the most done for the leader they serve are the ones who think, "I'm glad he or she was put in my path. I'm glad to be part of this. Serving in this way is the best way for me to reach my own goals."

Try a thought experiment to test out this approach. Imagine that you are an influential person in your organization or group and that I'm the new guy in town. I find a way to get introduced to you, and you have to decide what you think of me, whether you want to associate with me, and what you're going to say about me to your many colleagues, friends, and other connections. What do you want? First of all, you probably want to know if I "get" you—if I'll take you seriously, respect your feelings and your situation, and offer my sympathy and support. More than that, you've probably got some goal you're working on for yourself. Wouldn't you like it if I could help you toward that goal? But beyond all that, if you're going to accept me as your guide and leader, for an afternoon or for the rest of your life, you probably want to think, "Wow, this one is the real McCoy. He knows what he's doing." So the question is not: "How do I get my ambassadors to do what I want?" The question is: "How can I be the leader that makes others think, 'I'm glad he found me'?" And the answer is to be the kind of leader you would wish for—someone who has talent, integrity, honesty, and commitment. Someone who gives credit where credit is due and doesn't forget the people who helped him. Someone who inspires hope.

Those are lofty goals, but to work toward them it's enough simply to focus on staying true to your principles. I've found that when I do, there is a further benefit for me. If I become known for living by the rules in this book, then others may seek me out and try to associate themselves with me in business or in the community exactly because they feel that my values or my success will reflect well on them. My mentor in the practice of law, Jack Swarbrick, says that working to benefit others is actually a kind of "social capital" that you invest by seeming to give it away for free. The investment pays dividends when ambassadors and others decide that the best thing they can do for themselves is to find a way to work with you.

AMBASSADORS EXTEND YOUR SUCCESS

THE RIGHT AMBASSADORS CAN take you farther than you could believe possible, and the wrong ones can stop you in your tracks. I saw what a difference the right ambassadors make when I represented gospel star Fred Hammond. When I met Fred, he was already a success. He had played bass and sung with the Winans (the Jackson 5 of gospel), then joined the group Commissioned. Fred could sing, write songs, arrange them, and produce them. While he was still in the band, he also launched a solo career that we eventually brought to Verity Records. He was wonderful to his fans, generous with interviews, and he began racking up Grammy, Stellar, and Dove awards. Even so, writing, playing, and singing great songs wasn't the end of what Fred could do. He was creating a new genre of gospel music, but he would need the right ambassadors to do it.

In any religious service, whether in a church, synagogue, mosque, or wherever it may be, there is a part of the service set aside for acknowledging the goodness of God, for singing God's praises and offering worship and gratitude. This tends to be a highly traditional and "serious" part of the service, for example, when the old hymns are sung. Fred's innovation was to create music for the "praise and worship" portion of the service that was respectful of tradition, but to do it in a cutting-edge musical style. For the first time, praise and worship was being given fresh appeal for young people in the cities and for a more casual audience beyond the church context. To make an analogy to pop music, it was as if he had taken an old soul or R&B song from back in the day and created a dance remix that appealed to a whole new audience, but, of course, doing it with religious music had a special significance.

Fred was the first to pull it off with religious music, and he created a new genre: urban praise and worship. As my wife, Jennifer, describes it, this music makes you want to fall on your knees and cry out, "Holy, holy, holy!" They are songs that make you want to give yourself to the Lord. This more accessible music drew new listeners, both the young and the less devout, into one of the most important aspects of worship.

But even during the 1990s, as Fred became one of the most popular praise and worship leaders in the field, I could see that he hadn't reached his full potential. He was that rare artist who was also a visionary and a businessman, with the ability to take a concept and follow it all the way through. And at this point, when he began trying to realize the full scope of his vision for gospel, his efforts began to stall. The difficulty wasn't any lack of talent or personal commitment; it was the mismatch between his goals and his ambassadors.

Fred's life had not been easy, and after coming through hard times and betrayals, he had surrounded himself (as so many professionals do) with an inner circle of close family and longtime friends who had been with him from the beginning. But that approach, necessary in the rough, early days, began to hurt Fred as he grew more successful. Once, he was asked to appear in a concert, a worthy cause, but for less money than he had become accustomed to receive. I suspected he might do it anyway, as a blessing in the industry. But his manager took a hard line, angrily demanding more money as if Fred had felt insulted, and in the fight that followed Fred lost the chance to perform at that date entirely.

I was upset, and not just about the lost opportunity. Fred had a unique way of engaging people—though he was a big man, it was not his way to yell or intimidate. He was a quiet giant, mild mannered, a healer and a mender. When Fred handled a negotiation himself, even if you disagreed with him about how much he should get paid, you could still walk away feeling that he was a friend. But as his success grew, he could no longer handle every negotiation and arrangement himself.

There were fights over travel arrangements, about lighting design for his shows, and about the creative choices related to his sound. There were showdowns with record company executives with whom Fred had to keep working afterward. The ideas that Fred's people were fighting for were often fresh and exciting; had they been presented differently, people might have felt, "Wow, Fred is raising the style of this whole operation." But the way the disagreements were handled by his ambassadors left people telling one another, "You know what? Fred's a pain in the neck."

Beyond their interpersonal difficulties, Fred's ambassadors also lacked experience with the more complex business situations that his success now required. He was beginning to extend his reach in gospel, becoming a producer for other recording artists and investing in other ventures in the music business. He even built a recording studio. But as the scope of his operations grew, a number of the creative people in his inner circle—who did not share his gift for business or his larger vision for gospel—began to feel uncomfortable. There was jealousy and infighting among those who shared his creative gifts but had not developed an understanding of his larger vision for success in the industry.

For example, Fred and his inner circle shared an admiration for Sean "Puffy" Combs. They saw how Puffy hired a variety of different songwriters to work on his albums and then traveled around the country with them as part of a big, creative entourage. Like Puffy, Fred was drawing talented songwriters to his projects, and so a similar entourage formed around him. But the people handling his business concerns weren't considering the implications of putting all these songwriters and musicians on salary and letting them travel with Fred for long stretches of time. They could have been paid by the project, but instead they were receiving checks every month, whether they were writing songs with Fred or not. Not only was this arrangement a huge expense, it meant that he was surrounded by a large number of people, not all of them well known to Fred or especially loyal.

The bottom line was that people in his organization were imitating another artist's approach without considering whether that approach would help them reach their own long-term objectives, both creative and financial. I believe these ambassadors meant well, but they were having the opposite effect from what was needed:

1. Instead of building goodwill, they were damaging Fred's reputation.
2. Instead of creating opportunities for Fred to build new relationships, they were cutting relationships off.

3. Instead of promoting Fred's long-term interests and goals, their inexperience was holding him back.

4. Instead of carrying Fred's vision and style into the world, they were obscuring what he was all about.

When I stepped in, it was to offer Fred another approach. I told him that I understood how important it was to him to stay loyal to the inner circle that had been with him from the beginning and to take care of the people closest to him, but that it didn't make sense to give those people responsibilities they couldn't handle. At the same time, though, I told him that as his success kept growing, he couldn't be everywhere at once—booking his engagements, managing his office, representing his company, dealing with his staff. He needed ambassadors who could speak for him, who not only shared his vision but also conducted themselves as a reflection of his vision and his style. I wanted to help him understand that he was such an amazing person, he needed to hire people who would give the outside public the same kind of feel they would get if they dealt with him directly.

TAKE STOCK OF YOUR AMBASSADORS

TO HELP FRED SEPARATE his inner circle from his ambassadors, I asked a series of questions that I offer to anyone who is questioning whether they are being well served by those who speak for them.

1. List all the people you rely on to spread your message, whether as part of a formal business organization or a larger web of informal connections. Note what roles they're serving for you.

2. Make a list of the goals of your "operation," whether you are the leader of a formal organization or the center of an effort that is not yet formalized. What have been your strengths and weaknesses as you've worked toward those goals? In the case of

Fred Hammond, his organization was always good at creating ideas and seeking out opportunities, but not always as successful in following through with them. A lot of creative possibility and a lot of opportunity got lost along the way.

3. Compare the roles being played by your ambassadors. Who is able to do what you need to achieve your goals, and who needs to be given a different role better suited to his or her talents and experience?

4. As much as you can, take the emotion out of your decisions. It's always hard to tell people you've worked with that they're not doing what you need them to do and harder still to tell them that their role has to change. The most effective conversations are the ones without personal judgments, where you say: we all share the same goals, and we will reach those goals more effectively if we juggle the lineup.

When Fred and I had to tell people who had worked with him for a long time that he wanted them to serve in different ways, it was painful. Some recognized that they were not effective and chose to leave. Some he had to let go. Some took it well, some didn't. When my advice challenged a long-standing relationship, it was hard for him to reconcile at times. Some of his toughest-talking ambassadors didn't understand the new approach he wanted to take. They asked him, "Are you getting in bed with the record company? Don't you know that if you get too close you'll get hurt?"

I knew that to build his trust in my new approach, we had to start with smaller changes, so he could see what results we got. Slowly we made the bigger changes in his team. In time, his accomplishments began to grow in ways no one could doubt. Not only was he making more money, he was getting more exposure for his music and his religious message, and he helped to launch successful careers for other artists. His record company sought him out for musical concepts, marketing ideas, concerns about working in partnership with ministry, and guidance in resolving conflicts with their other artists. His influence and credibility grew. When DreamWorks decided to make *The Prince of Egypt,* the first major animated movie based on Biblical stories and intended for secular and religious families alike, they came to Fred for an understanding of the entire gospel music world as they developed the soundtrack—which would go on to win Oscars for best song and best musical score. Now he was helping to shape people's opinions of the whole gospel industry.

I helped Fred analyze his team in terms of his needs for ambassadors, but I think the growth in his career came most of all from an inner breakthrough. He began to rely more on himself and his own gifts. There's a myth out there that says if you don't want to be taken advantage of, you have to be tough and combative. But to me the thing that was amazing about Fred was his presence; often what he didn't say spoke louder than any tough talk. He could understand the need to stand up to his record company, for example, but also see that the reality of business is that no matter how adversarial a relationship might be in the beginning, once you close the deal it's a partnership. And in any kind of a partnership there is give and take. It was a proud day for me when I learned he was telling interviewers, "Max showed me how to get what I wanted without having to pound my hand on the table." When he trusted his own style and gifts, and surrounded himself with ambassadors who could follow his distinctive style of leadership, he took his success to new heights.

••••• CHAPTER EIGHT •••••

Remember Who **You** Are and Where **You** Come **From**

WHY IS IT THAT so many who achieve success later lose their way? It's as if one day they have the focus and the drive that they need, and then the next day, it's gone. As if they're racing at top speed, eyes on the road, but soon the motor cuts out and their attention wanders. At best, they roll on for a while as their momentum runs down; at worst, they wreck. But what did they lose that took them out of the race? And how can they get it back?

Of course, each of us has our own stories, with our own challenges, setbacks, and achievements along the way. But just as there are rules that can bring success to us all, there are also circumstances and misunderstandings that can prevent any of us from living according to those rules, day by day and year by year, until we reap their benefits. Almost all of those stories of falling short have something in common: along the way, we lost our inner sense of who we were and where we came from. That's when we made poor decisions. Sometimes it happened because we became discouraged or overwhelmed by the sheer intensity and endless demands of our lives; sometimes we lost the connection to our purpose; and sometimes it was success itself, or rather its trappings—the money, the things, the illusions of fame—that undermined our future success. In this chapter I talk about the reasons we sometimes lose our understanding of what makes us tick and the practices I rely on to maintain that understanding no matter what threatens it. There are three main dangers: becoming overwhelmed, losing connection to your purpose, and getting lost in success. Let's take them one at a time.

DANGER #1: OVERWHELMED AND DISCOURAGED

LIKE ANYONE, I'VE HAD my share of setbacks. As I mentioned in chapter 3, probably the biggest disaster of my entire career came in New York, when I worked as a consultant in the music business. My vision was to start a gospel division for an existing commercial record company, but I let someone unscrupulous get control of my business plan. He tried to implement it without me, going so far as to use my own list of contacts in the industry. To keep me out of his way, he even arranged to have my office moved to our company's basement.

So there I was, day after day. I had left Indianapolis, site of all my successes so far, and had come to New York City to find a stage for bigger achievements. Instead, I was a forgotten consultant in a basement office at a company whose executives barely knew I was there. Somewhere up above me, this other man who had the founder's ear was using my best ideas to advance his plan to become president of the company.

What had gone wrong? By that time in my career, I had achieved consistent success by knowing the market for African-American music and devising some unconventional methods for reaching our audience. That approach was the reason I had been brought in as a consultant. But this other executive, whom I'll call Richard, wasn't from my world. He had found success in marketing in another country and another business. The fact was that he had no relevant experience selling music to Americans. Every time I offered an idea, he said it wouldn't work. I knew that my approach worked fine, but Richard controlled a lot of the marketing resources in the company, and soon he was making it his business to block all of my projects. Eventually I was getting feedback from others in the company that Richard was trying to undermine my reputation, making remarks to throw doubt not just on my expertise but on my character.

In hindsight, the problem between us might seem clear. I had a new approach that he didn't understand, and so he was threatened by me. But I didn't try to understand our problem, I just took it personally. Whenever he made a proposal, I tried to prove him wrong. I never tried to see the logic behind his ideas because I already felt that I wanted to tear apart everything he said. In other words, I had forgotten my first rule. I wasn't listening to understand, I was only listening to come up with my next attack. My mind was full of resentment for what a bad time I was having in my new job.

Not only did I fail to learn what made Richard tick, I made the same mistake with my boss, the head of the company. I was so focused on my own irritation at Richard's lack of skills and ideas, I forgot to consider why he was hired. If he didn't offer my boss useful skills, what did he offer? Some kind of security? A personal friendship that was reassuring? There had to be something about my boss that made him want a man like Richard close by, but I never found out what it was. I was too busy trying to prove Richard wrong so the boss would send him away; but Richard didn't go away. Instead, he recognized that I didn't appreciate anything about him, and so he made it a point to stand in the way of the projects I wanted to do. That was how I wound up in the basement. Not only was I outmaneuvered, but I had gotten so distracted that I forgot myself and my principles. You name it: when it came to Richard, I forgot it.

How did I get out of that basement? The one thing I did do right was that I never called Richard out on what he had done. I never made a scene that would have convinced him to get me fired. Slowly, I got my personal resentment under control and started to get back to my usual approaches and routines. Then one day, a fresh opportunity came along within the company. My old assistant back in Indianapolis called to say that someone in the music business had seen my name on the liner notes of a CD and phoned me at my old law firm. The caller was hoping to get in touch with that album's producer. The funny thing was, the person calling actually worked at the same company where I was working as a consultant, but I was so unknown in the company that he didn't realize that the Max Siegel he was trying to reach in Indianapolis was actually downstairs. My assistant told me to go take a walk and find him.

At first, when I walked into his office, he seemed a little freaked out. I suppose it seemed as if I had just teleported halfway across the country to see him. But we struck up a conversation about the talented producer he had called about, and soon I discovered that this executive who called me had an amazing history of discovering great acts, both black and white. Like me, though, he was an outsider in the company, considered irrelevant by the young executives because he was older. We found that we shared a common misery—mediocrity was rampant in the company, and nobody would pay attention to us.

As we got to know each other, we recognized that we could get more done as partners than we could alone. We both "knew people who knew people," and in fact our lists of contacts overlapped. But the fact was, each of us could sell the other better than either could do for himself. "Why is Max spending all his time on that church music?" people would ask him, and he would answer: "Max? He's a great lawyer and he knows people all over the place, not just in music but in sports. What are you working on? You ought to talk to him." Similarly, people asked me: "Why do you hang around with that old guy?" And I would say, "I don't care how old he is, he's brilliant. Do you know some of the acts he discovered? And he's still doing it." We became each other's ambassadors.

On his advice, others in the company started coming to me for advice and to bounce ideas off of me. That was when I began to discover who in the company could help me get things done. He also helped me get credibility with the chairman, because they were friends from way back. In time, Richard's attempts to use my ideas failed, and who do you think got asked to fix what he had broken?

Once you know the whole story, the lesson might seem obvious: when I got so distracted that I forgot about my rules for success, success forgot about me. For a while, it was as if I had gotten stuck in a kind of personal "state of emergency" where the normal rules didn't seem to apply. It was a new job in a new city, where the situation wasn't what I expected. I lost my sense of who I was and how I operated. But when I got back to my rules, things changed. Instead of acting according to my momentary feelings, I worked toward my long-term goals. I found an ambassador who could help me get heard. I started using my outsider qualities—my background in the law and in sports—as advantages. And soon I found success again.

Maybe now you think you know what I'm going to say next: "The rules always apply." Sure, I could say that. I could go even further and say that exactly at the times you feel like you don't need them anymore, or you're impatient with them, that's when these rules are more important than ever. But although that's correct, I know that as a mentor I have to offer better help than that. It's not enough for me to say, "Try harder to live up to your principles." We've all heard that, and we've all, at times, fallen short. That's why, in this chapter, I want go beyond telling you to stick with these rules. I want to look more closely at the occasions when and the reasons why sticking with these rules becomes hard to do and the ways you can meet that challenge by reminding yourself who you are and where you come from.

Reduce the Pressure and Find Comfort in the Chaos

If people feel discouraged or overwhelmed enough, the rules they usually follow will fly out the window. In the hectic, provocative moment, we all forget what we meant to do or say, and sometimes we don't recognize the person who takes over the job of running our mouths or our actions. The goal, in those stressful times, is to reduce the pressure and manage the chaos enough so that you can hear your-self think—enough to remember who you are and how you make your best decisions.

This holds true no matter what kind of decisions you need to make—whether you're trying to solve the world's problems, land a corporate sponsor, or just deal with your own personal finances. If you try to handle everything at once, the sheer size and complexity of the task will overwhelm you. That's why, when I start to feel that there are too many things coming at me or that the challenges are too big, I try to respond with two steps. Together, they make almost any chaotic situation more manageable and easier to live with.

1. Build a mental framework to sort the demands on your time.
2. Invent a simple system to organize your work within that framework.

Let me start with an everyday example. Say I've had a long day and on my drive home I realize I still have phone calls to return—a whole lot of phone calls. Just listing them in my head is enough to make me wish I could put them off until tomorrow. Instead of trying to list them all, and instead of pushing the whole problem aside, I'll start to build my framework by asking myself: what categories do these calls fall into? That gets me started imagining a framework to manage the task.

Some will be "touch-base" calls, to check in with people I work with. I may need to find out how they're feeling or how far they've progressed on a given project. Others will be "creative" calls, to move forward with potential projects that I'm hoping to get started. The last calls will be "follow-up" calls, generally calls to people who want something from me, to let them know what progress I've made or what they can expect next. Once I have this framework, instead of a seemingly endless list of calls I have just three categories I need to handle.

Next I give myself a very simple organizational system: handle the categories one at a time. To start, I might get myself into a frame of mind to do just the creative calls. When I've crossed those off, I move on to the touch-base calls or the follow-up calls. That way I don't have to switch kinds of work often, which is draining; and as I finish with one of the three categories and move on to the next, I can see my progress clearly, which feels good.

For more complicated challenges, my approach is a little more complex, but only a little. I ask myself these general questions:

1. What's your mission? List your objectives. Now put them in order of priority.
2. What resources do you need to meet your objectives? Besides physical or financial resources, do you have the knowledge and skills to do the work yourself? If not, who can provide that extra "operational expertise"?
3. Can you sort the steps of the project into visual "buckets"? Give each one a label. Take them one at a time.

If you think about it, these three steps are the same ones I took in organizing my phone calls, only with the calls, resources were not an issue. I just identified the mission (returning my calls) and divided them into three "buckets" that I could handle one at a time. But as I'll show with some examples, this system, while simple, can help you manage some complex problems.

I apply this same approach to my day-to-day work life, even though my days are unpredictable. I travel weekly and I can't keep consistent hours, but even though I'll never be the kind of person who does the same thing at the same time every day, I still try to keep to the same daily routines. Some days I'm up before dawn and some days I'm sleeping off a night flight, but as soon as I can in the mornings, I do the same things in the same order, based on the approach I've just described. I check my e-mail, go through my snail mail, make a plan for the day, and so forth. The consistent routine is the stabilizing factor. It gives me some comfort and consistency even in the middle of chaos. That comfort and consistency, in turn, help me to keep my focus, to handle the setbacks and the times that feel nearly overwhelming by reminding me that I'm still the same person, with my reliable routines and my reliable rules.

Face Hard Times with Extra "Training"

In especially difficult times, I don't just create routines and plans; I take time to go back over them, revise them, and analyze them. If I'm feeling worried about a project, reviewing my plan and updating it can help me pinpoint what may be bothering me so I can work through it. In this way, even worry becomes a positive part of my process. Say that I can't sleep because I'm worried that a project isn't going right. I'll get up, go to my computer, and review my plan for the project, adding in new developments and concerns and revising the plan to take them into account. I hammer out my ideas and figure out the steps to my solutions. No matter what it might be, I like to put it on paper and make a flowchart or some other kind of visual so I can see how my solution could work. Even if I'm working on a financial plan for my family, I like to work it out on the computer, with graphics, steps to implement, explicit goals, and a budget. In that way I turn nervous energy and worry into productive preparation. Over time, this approach becomes a kind of ongoing professional self-development program, in which I give myself specialized "on-the-job training" based on the challenges I face.

When I suggest this kind of planning and revising, some people ask: Is that really necessary? After all, Max, you have a lot of experience already. Do you really need to be doing extra homework after all the success you've had? One of the things I learned from working with baseball great Tony Gwynn was that champions never stop being students. You might assume that champions are champions because they already know it all, but it's the other way around: they remain champions because they keep learning. In Tony's case, what a lot of people don't remember anymore is that by major-league standards, his natural athletic ability was only average. At the start of his career, he wasn't even drafted until the third round. But he made up for average ability by remaining a passionate and inventive student for his entire career: he became a champion because he out-prepared everyone else.

Known sometimes as "Captain Video," Tony was one of the first players to buy a video camera and have someone film his at-bats so he could study them afterward, which he did religiously. That first video camera cost him five hundred dollars back in 1983; ten years later, when he was already the top hitter in the game, he spent a hundred thousand dollars of his own money—more than many people spent then on a graduate degree—to build a custom videotaping facility in the San Diego Padres' clubhouse. He converted a storage closet in Qualcomm Stadium into his video library, and he shared the technology with his teammates so they could study every at-bat and every pitcher they faced. (When one of them was traded, he tried to hire Tony's videographer away to his new team, the Reds. The technician stayed loyal to Tony, though, and the player who had left, who no longer had the benefit of daily study of his batting performance, fell into a slump.)

What Tony was doing was a version of the three-step approach to handling challenges that I just described. He identified his *mission*, which was to become the best possible ballplayer he could be. He sought out the *resources* he needed to achieve his mission, which included the detailed video record of his choices against different pitchers and in different batting situations. He established a simple *routine*: review his batting performance after every game and study what pitchers threw him and what he did in response. Following this simple system, he compiled a mental encyclopedia of how pitchers behaved in every possible hitting situation and learned how he could best adjust his hitting to beat them.

In Tony's sixteenth season, he had put on some weight and was starting to go gray. While another player might have started easing toward retirement, he reviewed his video and realized he was in need of some additional "operational expertise"—that is, advice. He had a conversation with retired Red Sox batting legend Ted Williams, who helped him learn to start turning on inside pitches. Making use of his extra weight, not only did he maintain his extraordinary batting skill, but after fifteen seasons in which he was primarily known as a singles hitter, he blasted 17 home runs and 119 RBIs.

What these stories show is the power of remaining a student, no matter how much success you've had. Of course what you will need to study will vary with your work. For me, it's not a matter of watching video, but of mentally revising my business plans in light of what I've learned since the last "study session." Only you can say what it is you need to work on. The old expression says *practice makes perfect*, but I don't think perfection is the goal—you can never achieve perfect performance, and perfectionism as an attitude will just leave you frustrated. I would rather say: *practice makes permanent*. If you want to make success a permanent part of your life, you need to remember that you were once a beginner, and then keep practicing as if you're still starting out and eager to learn anything you can to do better tomorrow than you did today. It's another variation on the rule, *remember who you are and where you come from.*

Does this approach work if you're not Tony Gwynn, baseball hall-of-famer? Is it practical for the everyday demands of your life? It is. Early in my marriage, Jennifer and I were like a lot of young couples: we had a lot of debt. I wrote up a plan to get rid of it. I took on more speaking engagements, taught at a college for a semester, and found other side jobs in addition to my legal work. When the extra money started to come in, there were many ways we could have spent the money; but I reviewed my plan, remembered my goals and the reasons why I had set them, and we used that money to chip away at our credit card debts until we had paid them off.

And we didn't stop there. Once we were out of debt, I made a new plan to keep from taking on new debt. One goal was to pay for any vehicle we bought within one year. It was very satisfying to me to turn to Jennifer and say, "You see that car in the garage? We only owe $5,000 more on it." She would get this look of surprise and ask how that could be, and I would say, "Don't worry about it—I made a plan, and we got it done." I kept to that plan because I had it all spelled out—mission, resources, and practical steps I could see—and every day I could feel that keeping true to my plan moved me a little closer to where I wanted us to be.

When the Good Things in Life Are the Problem

Everyone knows that the demands and setbacks of work sometimes leave us overwhelmed or discouraged. What people don't talk about, though they should, is how the very prizes and comforts we all aspire to—the "finer things" we buy ourselves when we can—sometimes add to the stress in our lives. That's why from time to time I like to do a personal inventory of the things I've aspired to and what actual effect they're having on me. I start by making a list of the things "everybody wants" because—supposedly—they make our lives better. Some of those might be:

- A big house to live in
- A vacation home
- Great cars, boats, planes—even rockets, probably, for some people
- Travel
- Fine clothes
- Someone to help you clean or cook
- A nanny to watch the kids

When I have my list of the material things in my life that are demanding my money or my attention, I ask myself: OK, this item sure *looks* good, but is it improving my quality of life? When I pay for it and maintain it, am I satisfied, or is it just a source of headaches? Sometimes paying to have the house cleaned is actually a worse choice than cleaning it yourself. It's worth asking: are you really too busy to do that? In the same way, sometimes a boat is really nothing more than that old expression says: "a hole in the water into which you throw money." I go through each item in my personal inventory and consider whether it's improving my life or making it more complicated.

After I go through the things in my life that might make me feel overextended *financially*, I take a look at the things that make me feel overextended *emotionally*:

- Who are the people I'm trying to please? Must I please them all?
- What relationships are taking up my time? Are they healthy and beneficial, or are they draining me? Could I spend less time with some of those people?
- Am I getting caught up in gossip and idle speculation about people and events that don't really matter to me? I've learned that with all of the positive things I can do in my life, I can't afford to clutter my mind with negative chatter about people, no matter what they may have done. I ask myself: what if I stopped listening so much?
- What organizations am I working for? There are many reasons to be part of an organization. Some are good for networking, some provide knowledge, and some just make you feel good because you are doing something worthwhile. But like people, there are certain organizations that only take and give nothing back.

Once I have my list of the emotional commitments in my life, I note to myself which ones have benefits and which only add confusion and chaos to my life. Then I try to cut the harmful ones out. In this way I free up not just money but mental time and effort, and that lightens my load twice over, making it easier for me to keep my focus on my rules and the success they bring me.

Although I've been describing this as an inventory of your personal life, the same approach may also be valuable in your work life, depending on your job and your career stage. In some kinds of work, we have to take on whatever work we're asked to do and deal with anyone who comes through the door. But as we progress in our careers it may become possible to be more selective. These days, I only take on work where I feel I can make a significant contribution, whether that means settling a dispute, creating a business plan, growing a company, or opening up opportunities for others. I choose work in the areas I'm most passionate about and let the less compelling opportunities go by. In these ways, although I'm busier than I've ever been, I have greater control and greater satisfaction, and far fewer headaches than I would have otherwise. And that gives me the space and focus to remember my principles—even on the busiest days—and avoid the danger of becoming overwhelmed and discouraged.

DANGER #2: YOU LOSE YOUR CONNECTION TO YOUR PURPOSE

WHEN MY FRIEND AND client Reggie White retired from football in 1999, the Green Bay Packers honored him by retiring his jersey number. His career had been amazing. He was voted to thirteen consecutive Pro Bowl teams; he held the record for most sacks of the quarterback; on the business side he had helped lead the fight for free agency, helping him to become the highest-paid defensive player in the sport. Now finished with football, he turned to his work as a philanthropist, yet those of us who knew him knew he wasn't fully satisfied. He felt there was more he was meant to do. The next year, the Carolina Panthers lured him out of retirement with an offer of a million dollars to play one more season. When he retired again, he was voted by the NFL Hall of Fame to the NFL All-Time Team. This time he retired from football for real, at the height of his fame.

Many offers came his way, including product endorsements, a position as a television commentator at CBS, and speaking opportunities. He was asked to give a speech in front of the Wisconsin state legislature. His intention in that speech was to help the politicians understand the diversity of the body of Christ—that is, the community of Christian worshippers around the world. I knew Reggie, and I knew what he was trying to say, but he was not a speechwriter. The way he made his point caused uproar. In trying to show that Christians were a diverse group with diverse gifts, what he said was that Chinese people were so smart they could make watches out of televisions; that African-Americans were given the gift of dance; that Mexicans had the gift of family (they had twenty people living in the same house); and that Indians could walk on leaves so you couldn't hear them.

The response was pretty severe. He lost a number of his endorsements as well as his position at CBS. When I heard about it, my first, most practical thought was that he should have had someone review his speech before he gave it. But beyond that, I wished that a member of his inner circle had been there to help him address a deeper question about his purpose: he had such extraordinary gifts and he had done so much in sports, in the ministry, and in philanthropy, but was he sure he was meant to be writing speeches?

To complicate things even further, around the same time, his church burned down. Reggie raised money to rebuild the church, but later he found out that the cause of the fire had been arson; it had been set by a member of his own community, whom he had trusted. After these two events, Reggie became deeply discouraged. I felt I understood why: for most of his life, he had a strong sense of his purpose. As I described earlier in the book, he believed he had been given his astonishing physical gifts to serve a spiritual purpose. From the age of twelve, he knew he would be a football player and a minister. Now he could no longer play football, and at the same time his faith had been badly shaken. He left his congregation and became reclusive, studying Hebrew twelve hours a day with a rabbi so he could interpret the word of God himself. There were rumors among some newly Christian football players that he had converted to Judaism or that he had gone crazy.

It was terrible for me to see a friend go through what he went through. It was also a powerful reminder of how lost any of us can get when we lose the connection to our purpose. What does the word "purpose" mean? It's another of those words like "vision" or "influence" that is often discussed, but rarely in a practical way. I think of it this way: each of us has passions, those yearnings that fuel our visions and give our life meaning. We also have to meet the practical requirements of our lives, to take care of business, pay the bills, and fulfill our obligations to others. Many people I've mentored have faced a crossroads, where passion and practical obligation seem to be signs pointing in opposite directions. I saw it in my work with aspiring singers and musicians, how those who have strong a connection to their passions, such as artists or others drawn to a particular *kind* of work, often try to solve this problem by acting as if passion is all that matters. *I'm a singer; I love to sing, so I was meant to sing no matter what the outcome.* Then there are those who see their purpose as achieving material success by whatever means, and who treat passion as dispensable. For them the danger is that the efforts needed to maintain their success, and even their success itself, will come to feel empty.

How do you resolve the tension? I believe we are provided with signs of our true purpose: if you have the gifts and talents to do something very well, that is a sign that you are meant to do it. In practical terms, then, to find your purpose, or to recover your connection to it when it is lost, you need to follow your passions but keep your eyes open. Observe where you do your best work, where you have the most impact on others, and where you feel the most satisfied. You will find your purpose revealed in those areas of overlap, where your passion brings you practical success—though that success may not come where you expected it. Instead of choosing between what you love and what you need to do to take care of business, look for the ways to combine them. Purpose is a kind of compass, pointing the direction of your path even if you can't always see every twist and turn clearly ahead of you.

In chapter 2, I talked about vision—not a dazzling Hollywood production with angels singing in the background, but a practical goal you can see ahead of you, that shows you how to move in harmony with your purpose. For me, starting out, it was decent clothes and shoes that would prevent people from prejudging me because I was poor. For Reggie, it came when he was twelve and he told his mother he was going to be a minister and a football player. That vision showed him how to live in harmony with his purpose for many years. But the day came, as it does for most of us, when the vision he relied on no longer showed him the way ahead. At that point, often in frustration and sadness, we must get back to basics: what makes us tick?

For most sports lovers, that moment comes much sooner. Most of us never become professional athletes, but if we're fortunate we find other ways to stay close to that passion. In racing, teams hire over twenty-five different categories of worker, from accountants to mechanics. Every one of those jobs offers a fan the opportunity to combine passion with practical work. So just because your passion doesn't lead you straight to a career, that doesn't mean you give up on it, either.

What made the difference for Reggie White? He was living in Charlotte after his retirement from the Carolina Panthers and he became intrigued with stock car racing. Joe Gibbs, the head coach of the Washington Redskins, had retired from football and focused his attention on his NASCAR team, Joe Gibbs Racing, where his son, the driver J. D. Gibbs, was now the president. They had a diversity initiative within their team, and when Reggie saw what they were doing he agreed to contribute some money to bring people of color and women into the sport. As his involvement grew, he got interested in starting a bush team, comparable to a minor league team in baseball, to be the first African-American–owned team in NASCAR racing. He asked me to get involved.

The story of our attempts to buy a team, first in the bush league and then at the top level, is long and complex, and twice we had to suspend our efforts out of respect for tragedies. First, a plane crash killed many of the people we were negotiating with to buy the bush league team. Second, only weeks before we closed a deal to buy a team at the Cup level, Reggie himself died suddenly. That plan had to wait until I became president of DEI, when I bought the team we had wanted, Ginn Racing, on behalf of Teresa Earnhardt, and merged it with DEI.

But although our plans didn't go according to plan, and success took a form none of us expected at the start, from that first phone call, that new vision of helping to bring greater diversity to NASCAR helped restore Reggie to a sense of purpose and an enjoyment of life. From our first phone call about it, I could hear that he was throwing off his discouragement and sounding more like the man I knew. He was fired up about racing as a sport and about the possibility that he could make room for people of color to succeed, as he had done in football and in his work as a minister and philanthropist. It was terrible to lose him, but I'm grateful that at the end of his life, he had escaped the danger of living out of harmony with his purpose.

DANGER #3: YOU LOSE YOURSELF IN SUCCESS

THE THIRD RISK TO your ongoing success lurks where you might least expect it: in success itself. Of course, success is much better than the alternative, but I've seen how hard it can be for people to keep their focus and their sense of who they are when success finally arrives. Money can do it and so can fame—and of course, the two often go together. But their specific risks are different, so I'll take them one at a time.

The Risks of Money

Someone gets a big promotion, lands a big client, closes a big deal, or just comes into more money, and suddenly a change comes. You can hear it in their attitude and see it in their behavior. For some, it's a dramatic shift of personal focus. "I have arrived," they seem to say, and their attention shifts all at once from others to themselves. They start to feel that they are far more important than they ever realized, and their humility, compassion, attention to detail, and caring all seem to fly away, replaced by a sense of grabby entitlement. They focus on things that have nothing to do with the true essence of who they are, yet they treat those material things as the only real essentials. They are all about the material things they can't live without, the places where they have to be seen, and the new crowd they have to be around. People who used to know them don't recognize them anymore.

For others, financial success brings numbness. That was how it was for me for a while when I was still single, working as a lawyer and doing very well by any outward standard. I remember once I went back home for a visit and saw the mother of a friend I had grown up with. She said, "I'm so proud of you, Max! You always said you would be a millionaire by the time you were thirty, and you're doing it!" Now, it might seem as though that would have been one of the proudest moments of my life, but to be honest—and I know this might sound strange—when she said so, I didn't feel much. I had probably expressed that financial goal to her sometime as a kid, but I didn't even remember saying it. And while it was true that I was setting career goals for myself and reaching them, somewhere along the way I stopped feeling the satisfaction. I had even begun to ask myself: why did I go into such a demanding career? Why was I working so hard? My big achievements felt small, and the small setbacks felt huge. On paper I looked like a success, but inside my life felt like it was actually getting worse. I hardly knew who I was anymore.

What was the problem? Hadn't it been one of my goals my whole life to achieve financial success? Yes, but now that I was reaching that goal I had to face a deeper question: what was behind those financial and career targets? Sure, I was an overachiever, but why? The truth was, deep down, many of my "goals" were really fears: I was afraid to be poor again, afraid that when I had kids they might have a child-hood like the one I had known—a struggle to survive that was hardly a childhood at all. That fear gave me an almost obsessive drive to suc-ceed, but in the places it drove me I forgot the boy I used to be, the one who had sworn to make a better and more stable life. He had never sworn to found a law firm, to bill hundreds of hours a year to clients, or to maintain an ever more expensive lifestyle. The money and the career were always the means to an end: a life free from violence and poverty, where I could make a family that was safer, more loving, and more open to the world's opportunities than what I had known. That was what made me tick. The money was only a part of it.

The Risks of Celebrity

Although my roles in music and sports have been mostly behind the scenes, not in the spotlight, I've experienced increasing public attention. Whether I'm at a music conference or at the track, I'm al-ways asked for autographs. Our favorite restaurant in Charlotte offers "Max Siegel Homemade Crab Cakes" on their menu. One day, my wife was reading an article in *Ebony* magazine and found this descrip-tion of contemporary life for African-Americans: "[We live] in an age of seeming parity, where Condi Rice can become secretary of state, Oprah Winfrey can make the Forbes 100 list and businessman Max Siegel can head up DEI, the number one franchise of NASCAR, that good old boy bastion of car fanatics. . . ." When Jennifer read that, she called out, "Max, you're not going to believe this!"

Frankly, at times it is hard for me to believe. But what I don't accept, and what I encourage people to fight against, is this illusion that someone with "celebrity status" in a certain area is not the person he or she used to be, maybe not even a person at all, just some kind of different, special thing that you can't talk to, or only talk to in a certain stylized way. The fact is, my own success in working with stars of music and sports has come, in part, because celebrity doesn't impress me so much. All kinds of people come to me for advice or help with their problems, and what I've found is that the stars have problems just like everyone else's. They're upset about their taxes or they're fighting with their girlfriend or boyfriend or spouse. They wish they were better appreciated or that they could make more money or have more time to themselves. They may conduct their professional affairs on a different scale than some people, they may throw a lot of money around, but their personal lives aren't all that different in the ways that count. If anything, I've found that the biggest names are likely to have more problems, with more coming at them at once, and they find, quite frankly, that what sets them apart from other people is just that they're more lonely and miserable.

But for the most part, I've been blessed to stay levelheaded about money and fame, and I attribute a lot of that to my mother. She would always let me know in a heartbeat, no matter what I might have accomplished, that to her I was still the person I always was. She would say, "I don't give a —— who you are or what you're doing, or what kind of education you have or what title. Every man puts his pants on one leg at a time."

Sometimes I felt that she picked at me when I did something good, maybe as a way to keep me from getting carried away. That's not a technique I would use to achieve that goal, but if I could give one piece of advice to every successful client I've ever had, and to myself as well, I would say: get up every morning and look in the mirror. Don't look at your new clothes or your new hairstyle or any of that. Look at your face. It will be the same face as yesterday, just a day older. You may have a certain salary or a particular job, you may be this person's spouse or that person's parent, but none of it changes who you are deep down. You're the same person you were yesterday, only with more responsibilities.

How did I lose that numbness I described? The satisfaction in life returned for me when I met and married Jennifer. We had dated in college, and I had known her even back in high school—she understood what I had come through, and for that reason sharing my successes with her reminded me what it was all for. Through her I discovered where I feel most successful and where my efforts feel most worthwhile. It's not flying on a company jet. It's not in the green room, waiting for my next television interview. I do feel it when I'm wearing a fine suit, because I remember the irregular clothes I used to wear with the crooked seams and other defects out there for anyone to see, but the clothes were always more a symbol and a means, not the real goal.

I feel success most strongly when I'm with my family and I can see the world we're making through our children's eyes. I remember how my sons came to me when they were six and four, and asked me if God was compassionate: "Daddy, does He care about us?" What touched me was how they were able to explore their own emotions for themselves and to frame a question about God. I can't remember ever thinking that way as a kid—I was just keeping it moving, trying to make sure my little sister and I got by. For me, the dream of success was always a dream of building a home that was safer, more loving, and more open to the world's opportunities. Now for me there's nothing more rewarding than to hear how openly my kids encounter the world, to hear their questions and to look into their eyes.

BALANCE YOUR PAST SELF AND YOUR FUTURE SELF

CONNECTIONS TO FAMILY ARE one of the most powerful ways I remind myself who I am and where I came from. Now I want to describe other ways that work for me, as examples of how you can find the reminders that will work for you. Does it surprise you that I would recommend gathering reminders of your past? After all, back in chapter 2 I talked about the importance of seeing where you want to be, not where you are or where you've been. That's true, but now we need to refine that rule. Because although the secret to *reaching* success is to see where you want to be, the secret to *keeping* success is to stay grounded, even as you move forward, in where you came from.

Why? Like almost everything in this book, it comes back to maintaining mutually beneficial relationships. In this case, the relationship I mean is the one between two of your most important clients: your future self and your past self. The teenager I was back in the Indianapolis ghetto needed to connect with his future self, to have the vision of what he could be that gave him direction and hope. But while the teenager needed that dream of success, the successful man he became needs to remember the teenager in the ghetto, or all he'll have is endless striving for material gain and celebrity, which is a recipe for losing yourself. The solution, at every stage of life, is to establish that balance between the person you've always been and the places you're trying to go.

One essential habit that reminds me who I am and where I came from is also one of the most straightforward: for most of my adult life, even when my work has been based in New York or in Charlotte, I've kept a house in Indianapolis. I still get my hair cut at the same barbershop where I've gone for more than twenty years. The shop is in a little strip mall, three stores in a row on the main drag in Indianapolis, in an area that's not totally rundown but not great, either—it's somewhere in the middle. On one side of the barbershop is a liquor store where people show up in the morning as soon as the doors open. On the other side is a tax preparation place that's only open during tax time. Across the street there's a Laundromat and a fish market where people go for lunch.

The barbershop has a sign in the window—"Fresh Kutz"—that's so old the paint is chipped. The price of a haircut is written on a dry-erase board, and there's a big homemade bench that can fit fifteen people sitting and talking while they wait for their turn in one of the four barber chairs. Thanks to the movies *Barbershop* and *Barbershop 2*, many people now know that in the black community, a barbershop is much more than the place you get your trim. It's the social hub where everyone in the community goes to exchange news, catch up on what's going on, and tell stories. When I go there, I see a lot of the same people I knew growing up.

But how does going to my old barbershop help me keep my connection to myself? When I've gotten my hair cut and I've talked to the old guys and the others in the community, am I refreshed, restored, and renewed? No. Nothing like that. It's not a spa. When I come out again, I don't feel any different than when I went in. And that's why I treasure it. To me, what's so important about going back is that it prevents me—I could say it protects me—from experiencing the crazy highs of success, money, and fame, and then the crashes and the need for recovery that I've seen so many others go through. I may have flown into Indianapolis that morning in business class, but I feel the same way I did when I drove up in a '78 Ford LTD. What's special about that place is that being there, and talking to the people I've known in the way I've always known, doesn't feel special. It feels normal. I feel normal. And that's the point.

Back when I was digging through the bins to find a decent shirt at the Cash Bargain Center, I never felt inside myself that I was any less than anyone else or different in any way that really mattered from people who could afford the finest clothes. I always wanted to be judged for who I was. I didn't need to arrive in a Porsche for people to say I was cool. I just hoped that I could dress in a way that took away people's distractions and excuses, so they would judge me on my merits. Now that I can wear a fine suit or drive an expensive car when I want to, I need to remember that I'm still the same man inside as I was in my Cash Bargain Center days. To me, most of the trouble people get into comes when they're trying to be something other than who they really are. I go to the barbershop for the haircut, for the people, and to make sure that when I come out I remember that I'm the same man I always was.

LIST AND REVIEW YOUR PRIVATE REMINDERS

MY APPROACH IS NOT for everyone. Not everyone needs to make a literal trip back home. Some of the old neighborhoods are gone now, and some people who could go back tell me, "Oh no, Max, I don't want to go there." But it's not the physical travel that makes the difference. The visit is just one way to remember who you are. The question is: what will remind you? What memories or habits are so powerful that you can go back to them, like a deep well, and draw out what you need, no matter what else is happening in your life? It reminds me of something my friend John Carter often says: "I may live in the suburbs, but I'm still from the street."

1. Find your private triggers. What brings you back? You might need to call up an old friend, look over family pictures, or go through some of the mementoes you have in storage. Sometimes that sense of roots comes back watching certain movies or rereading books. If you don't have a reliable method, then experiment and note to yourself what works for you.

2. Recall the important personal lessons you have learned. When my father was dying of cancer at the Mayo Clinic, he wrote me a letter about discovering, at that last moment, what mattered

to him. It wasn't a sappy apology letter; it was his attempt to share what he had learned so that I could make use of it. I still had a chance. He said that he hadn't appreciated the world in front of him, the grass growing outside his hospital window, the trees and flowers—the simplest things. What stayed with me most was that he said he had only just learned to appreciate a glass of water. When I'm at risk of getting caught up in the hoopla, I look at a plain glass of water and think of him, discovering gratitude.

3. Keep your own image of happiness and satisfaction. The more success you have, the more people will try to convince you that they know what you want, and the more resources you will have for acquiring things that you don't need to begin with. When I think over the happiest times in my life, the memories I come back to are often the simplest moments of my childhood. I remember playing hide-and-seek in the yard, or stickball in the alley with a broomstick for a bat and pork-and-beans can for a ball. Somehow those simple times with family and friends are the ones I treasure most. I've come to see that the worst thing that ever happened to me, being born poor, was in this one way the best, because I learned to be happy poor, and so I know what happiness is.

4. Return to your spiritual home. Worship isn't just inspiring; it reminds me that I aspire to become a more complete Christian, to deepen my relationship with God. It's a lifetime commitment, one I don't always understand, but which reminds me who I am and what I hope to become.

5. Remember that tomorrow is not promised to any of us. If you keep your eyes open, you will see people who appear to have it all wake up the next day with nothing. The blessings we hope for can be taken away in an instant. I think of that to remind myself to appreciate what I have, and to stay true to what got me where I am today.

I've listed the reminders that work for me, but of course the important question is what works for you. Take a few minutes now to list the personal examples that my list may have helped bring to mind. Which people, places, and memories restore your sense of yourself? How could you check in with them more often? Commit to establishing one new routine that brings you in contact with your most powerful reminders—even if it's something as ordinary as choosing where to get your hair cut.

IN THIS CHAPTER, I'VE described three different ways that people lose sight of who they are and where they come from: by becoming overwhelmed and discouraged, by losing connection to purpose, and by getting lost in the trappings of success. Yet while the specific causes may vary, the essential problem is the same: we get lost in the worries and pressures of our lives and in all the hoopla around success, and then we lose our focus on the rules and practices that built our success in the first place. The solution is to clear away the clutter, turn down the noise, and ask yourself, regularly, who am I? Where do I come from, and how do I stay true to the purpose that brought me here? The answers to those questions are truths we feel within us, and they are our most reliable guide to a successful and satisfying life.

Consider three recent U.S. presidents: Ronald Reagan, Bill Clinton, and Barack Obama. We may disagree with their ideologies and argue the merits of their policies, but an amazing number of people will concur that, as we got to know all three men, we could feel who they were and what they stood for. They reached their success by knowing who they were and being able to connect with people all over the country based on that truth. And though they had to play the game of politics, they played it for the sake of a deeper purpose each of them felt, a purpose that didn't change with the political winds. To me, they are examples of what you can do when you know who you are and where you came from.

I saw the same consistency in the choices made by Reggie White and Tony Gwynn over the decades. I remember when Reggie was about to sign his big, multiyear contract with the Green Bay Packers. I asked him: are you comfortable with a long-term commitment? Because someone else could come along next week and negotiate a bigger deal, and then you wouldn't be the highest paid defensive player anymore. He said, "Oh yes, I'm comfortable. I love this team and I want to win the Super Bowl with them." For Reggie, it wasn't about making the most money he could make. He had a long-term relationship with his team and his sport and his community. The money was just a part of it.

Tony Gwynn, too, chose to stay with one team for many years—he played for the Padres for seventeen seasons—because he wanted more than the money: he wanted a good quality of life for his family, he wanted to stay close to the loyal fans who had supported him for years, and he was committed to the team and the success of the younger players, not just to himself. Over the years, we watched some players price themselves out of the market, but Tony stayed where he was valued, stayed relevant to the team, and made a graceful transition to the coaching staff when he reached the end of his playing days. He was true to the baseball life he wanted for himself, not to maximizing his earning potential, but it's possible that in the long run he made more money too, because he stayed valuable to his team even after his physical abilities diminished.

Over the years, I've come to believe that whoever any of us are, when we're quiet in a room, alone, we all want the same things:

- A decent quality of life
- The chance to improve the lives of those we care about
- Mental peace
- Harmony with our purpose
- Recognition for our positive contributions
- Enough structure and accountability in our lives that we can feel we're making progress

You can have those things whether you're turning the lug nut in the plant or running the company, because more than anything, they depend not on reaching this or that benchmark of material success, but on living by these rules, making your commitments for the long run, and valuing the relationships that give our lives meaning.

••••• CHAPTER NINE •••••

Change Their Minds and
Uplift the Community

PEOPLE GET IT BACKWARDS. They think step one is *doing for yourself,* and only later, when you've got that mastered, can you try a little of step two, *doing for others.* Of course, it's great when the successful give back to the community—I always try to encourage and recognize that kind of community uplift. But my success and the success I hope for you comes from changing people's minds as you go, doing for others first and succeeding along with your partners and your community. When you work by knowing what makes other people tick, then changing people's assumptions and benefiting the community are not just the icing on the cake. They can get you the whole cake.

However, I understand that when your mind is set on making a living or fulfilling your personal responsibilities, then "changing their minds" might seem beside the point. "Uplifting the community" might sound like a far-off goal, the sort of charity work that only the rich or the unimaginably selfless have time to take on. Too many people mistake these for goals you can't achieve until you have more money or more power in your organization, yet what I've found is that it works the other way around: it's by changing people's minds and uplifting the community that you reach success. The opportunities are right there, all around you—if you can help others to see them. When you do, the organizations you work for will solve more problems, your business will grow more quickly, and your work will become easier and more meaningful to you. Let's take these three benefits one at a time.

MOST INNOVATIONS AND SOLUTIONS COME FROM BELOW

WHEN A BUSINESS OR other group solves a problem or makes a measurable improvement, there is usually someone with a title who steps forward to thank the people involved. Often it sounds then as if that person—the manager, the team leader, the head of the project, the president—must have been some kind of genius, planning it all out and making it happen. When I was younger, it often sounded that way to me, so it came as a surprise when I discovered that the people in charge in almost any organization rarely bring about positive change on their own. Most of the great new ideas and solutions to problems—big or small—come from below and are made possible by people who have to change a lot of minds (often including the minds of their bosses) before their good ideas can succeed and benefit the community.

I discovered this for myself in my first job out of college. I worked as a department supervisor for General Motors, supervising two enormous warehouses that shipped GM auto parts all over the world. We had a problem: we were falling behind on our shipments. Our customers would place orders through a central computer; it was my department's job to collect the parts they had ordered (everything from spark plugs to entire hoods), pack them for safe travel, and ship them out to the car dealers and auto parts franchises. The trouble was, we couldn't handle the volume of orders. We fell two months behind, which meant a lot of unhappy GM customers around the world who couldn't get their cars repaired because they were waiting on our parts.

I learned a lot, trying to solve this problem. The first thing I learned was that while I might be "department supervisor," I couldn't

solve the problem myself. Yes, I understood that we needed to rear-
range how we stored all the parts in our warehouses, so we could get
to what we needed faster and streamline the process of lining everything up and packing it for shipment, but I couldn't figure out how to
do it. I assumed that was because I didn't have an engineering degree.

The next thing I learned was that the people who did have engineering degrees were the ones who had designed the pick-pack-and-
ship system we already used—the system that wasn't fast enough. The
engineers and higher-level managers at the company couldn't explain
to me why we were so far behind on our orders, but as far as they were
concerned, they had already done their job and the system was fine.
They weren't going to help me change it.

I came to realize that the people who knew the most about the
problem were the people who actually worked in the plant, the workers I supervised. Many of them had worked there for twenty or thirty
years and they knew exactly the distance you had to go to get a certain
part and how best to fill the bins for wrapping and shipping. So could
I just use my authority as supervisor and order them to find a more
efficient system?

As I discovered, the answer to that was also no. The culture of the
union workers at that time was that you did your job, you didn't think
about it. Punch in at 6:30, do what you're told, punch out at 2:30, and
you're done. In addition, the history of the relationship between management and the union workers in the auto business had always been
adversarial and tense, going back to the long, sometimes violent strikes
that had forged the union. And on top of that history, there was a further division based on education: the union workers had high-school
educations, while supervisor positions like mine now required college degrees. For all of these reasons, as far as most of the people who
worked for me were concerned, thinking about larger departmental
problems was not in their job description. And while in another organization, I might have been able to offer bonuses to those who helped
me, that was not how things were done back then in the auto industry.

In other words, I needed the help of the people who worked for me, but I quickly learned that although my title was "supervisor," all I had to change their minds was my collection of rules about what makes people tick. So I got back to basics. I spent as much time as I could talking to the workers, getting to know their situations and their concerns. Gradually I found some ambassadors. One was a woman who was married to a supervisor and could see both sides, union and management. Another was a very talkative line leader who had a lot of ideas about how things could run better, but no one who would listen to him. Another was a very grumpy, quiet guy, nicknamed Smiley, whom everyone thought was a loner, but who turned out to want to participate in the life of the shop.

As I got to know them and earned their trust, I found that many of the workers were frustrated with the way their jobs were organized. The current system kept them under constant pressure to speed up their work, which was very stressful. I tried to show them that I shared their frustration and that I didn't see the situation as union versus management or noncollege versus college. Instead, I felt we were all human beings who could benefit if we could do our jobs without that constant pressure to make up for lost time and late orders.

As they got to know me and my approach, several of my employees were willing to sit down together and make suggestions for rearranging the parts in the warehouses and changing the systems for packing up the bins so we could get them out the door more quickly. None of them had engineering degrees, but they had plenty of practical experience. It took us three weeks to redesign the system and implement the new approach, and then we started to see results. Six weeks later, we actually got ahead of schedule.

From that first job in manufacturing, I learned that improvements don't usually come from the top down. Often it's the person who lacks the authority but has the knowledge or creativity who can see the steps to success for the whole community and has to work to change minds to get there. I've seen the same truth among my colleagues in the law, though legal work couldn't be more different from the GM plant. For example, when the recession hit in 2008, many law firms, like businesses of all kinds, found that they could no longer count on the flow of new clients that had always sustained them. In some fields, professionals realized quickly that they would have to market themselves more aggressively, but the law had always been a "gentlemanly" profession, and many were wary of advertising and other forms of self-promotion. There were formal ethical restrictions on what a law firm could say about itself—for example, you couldn't promise results—but beyond that, there was an established culture that distrusted self-promotion and resisted even internal methods, such as brand studies, that discover and highlight what it is about your company that a customer might value.

This culture of gentlemanly restraint was strongest among the senior partners, who of course had most of the power. The result for a few firms I knew well was that even as business worsened and billable hours declined, the senior partners resisted learning more about ways to work around the rules on how firms could solicit business. Some younger attorneys became so frustrated that they left to start their own small boutique firms, taking additional business away with them. It fell to the younger attorneys left behind to become ambassadors for a new kind of dialogue: to educate their firm about what made their clients tick and how to do business in ways that respected the special nature of the legal profession but also got the firm's name out.

One new approach was for firms to become more active in their surrounding communities. They began to sponsor social events and camps for kids. They started making firm presentations at seminars. For example, a firm that did construction law joined the green building association, to become part of the movement toward environmentally sound construction. By making a presentation on environmentalism and law at an industry conference, they could benefit the construction community while getting to know potential clients who could use their skills. They offered related information on their Web site and in Web-based seminars.

Another approach was to launch a small public relations campaign by letting reporters and bloggers know about members of a firm who could provide expertise on a subject for stories or blog posts. A third approach was to make use of social media such as Twitter; it turned out that just as on television, the daily drama of certain kinds of lawyers was compelling to many people. Again, none of these new approaches came about by order of those in charge; they came from below, as younger, less-powerful attorneys showed that there were ways to win clients' attention and interest without appearing to be shameless ambulance-chasers.

I said in chapter 7 that knowing what makes people tick is at heart an approach to leadership. From the moment you first try to see where someone else wants to be and how you can get there together, you are a servant-leader, helping to show them the way. Now I want to add: the essential *act* of the servant-leader is to change people's minds in order to uplift them and their community. Every negotiation I've described in this book was an attempt to change someone's mind by helping him or her to see the possibility of a joint benefit— in other words, a way to benefit a larger number of people than just one. Sometimes a community is only a community of two people, but more often than not, that benefit will require a change of thinking in the larger group. That's why changing people's minds isn't a sideline. It's the main game.

BECOME AN AMBASSADOR FOR A NEW DIALOGUE

WHETHER THE MINDS YOU want to change are few or many, whether the community you want to uplift is big or small, you need to become an ambassador—not an ambassador between two people or two groups, but an ambassador between an idea or approach and the people who could benefit from it if they understood it better. Whether you need to change people's practical approach or their feelings, the basic steps are the same:

- **First, change your own assumptions about why people don't talk.** In the work of changing minds, start with yourself. Consider why the people you need to work with may not be communicating yet. Most times, people don't talk because they don't understand what they can offer each other. Over time, as the habit of not talking gets established, misunderstanding starts to feel inevitable. People come to believe that their silence and separation is the result of differences that can never be changed, but usually it's only a lack of open communication.

- **Identify the assumptions that hold people back.** Often you can discover those assumptions when people suddenly start telling you what you "can't do," what is impossible or not worth trying. You can't get union workers to collaborate with management. You can't market a law firm without destroying its traditional standards. These people can't get along with those people. When you hear "can't," you know where the organization may need your help.

- **Start a safe dialogue.** Usually, the people who most need to communicate are the ones least likely to do so, not because they are hopelessly different or poisoned with hatred, but because they are uninformed or afraid. The fear is that talking will be awkward and uncomfortable; the information they lack is how it will benefit them to try. Rather than addressing these concerns head-on, treat those whose minds you need to change like someone alone at a gathering who needs to make a first connection. Listen to understand what would be comfortable first subjects of conversation—some shared passion or similar experience or goal. When they start to relax and listen to your ideas, usually they will wind up discovering—shockingly enough—that they can find more in common with your thinking than not.

- **Move the conversation from what you already have in common to what you could accomplish together in the future.** Once you find similarities, then you can try talking about shared frustrations and shared goals. In this way, the promise of uplifting the community prepares people's minds to open and to change.

- **Trust that despite their surface differences and their sometimes strong emotions, people's motivations are basically the same.** When they feel comfortable, and when new ideas or opportunities are presented to them in terms of their needs and interests, pretty much everyone will make decisions the same way. I'm reminded of this every time I see someone drinking bottled water. Who would have believed a generation ago that people would pay for plain water like it was a soft drink? I'm sure that many marketing experts assumed water couldn't be sold—until someone got close enough to their audience to learn how it served their needs. The question is always how well you know what makes your target audience tick. Have you observed their behavior closely enough? Have you found the way to reach out to them and meet their needs?

- **If there are charged emotional topics to be resolved, save them until you are already having success together.** If there are grievances that need to be resolved or old behaviors that need to be changed, wait until you can discuss them in terms of making a good relationship even better. In this way, benefit to the community smoothes the way for opening and changing minds. This approach works equally well whether the obstacle is a practical business problem or an emotional history. How can that be? The explanation is that there are very rarely problems in business that don't spring in part from strongly held feelings, and there are few strongly held feelings that don't have at least some basis in a practical problem. The practical and the emotional are always intertwined.

WHEN STRONG FEELINGS ARE THE OBSTACLE

I'VE GIVEN TWO EXAMPLES already of practical business problems that hid assumptions that were holding the community back. Now I want to look at an example that shows the reverse, a situation where strong community feelings hid deeper business opportunities. When I first worked in the music business, I discovered that there were actually two separate businesses in America selling Christian religious music. Although it was not often discussed, religious music was segregated—the term "Christian music" meant Christian religious music by and for whites, and the term "gospel music" meant Christian religious music by and for blacks. Many black artists felt pushed to the margins, their albums confined to special stores that catered to black customers, excluded by the larger, white music industry and unable to succeed financially. While some of this was fading history, some was ongoing—for example, there was a movement to remove the word "gospel" from the name of the Gospel Music Association and replace it with the word "Christian," on the grounds that the organization didn't include black gospel music and shouldn't. This very unchristian separation between the two forms of Christian music was not just very old, it was considered something you couldn't discuss.

To some, that might have been a discouraging situation, but I didn't see it that way. Instead, I tried to focus on the opportunity to change minds and uplift the musical community. I started by questioning my own assumptions about why these two groups didn't communicate. Yes, this division between "gospel" and "Christian" was old, but perhaps its age meant that it was nearly worn out. The two sides didn't talk, but the fact that people don't talk doesn't prove there are irreconcilable differences. Usually, it just means that the people involved don't want to feel uncomfortable. So if the problem was that no one would talk, then the question was: how to start the conversation? What would draw them out?

As usual, I got back to basics. I said to myself, all right, I'm standing between these two sides that don't work together and can't even talk about it. I was the first African-American president of a record label of this kind, but that didn't give me any special authority or power over the other record companies; they had their own presidents and none of them took orders from me. I realized that I couldn't take charge, but I could become an ambassador for a new, more comfortable dialogue.

What did the two sides have in common? If nothing else, they were in the record business. They all wanted to sell more music. So my approach to defusing the historical sensitivities, establishing trust, and helping the two sides start appreciating each other was to put aside race and just talk business. I would meet another president of a record label and I would talk about what was on his mind. What kind of return on investment were they seeing for different acts? How much did they spend on variable marketing? Were they having more trouble these days getting their records played on the radio? Well, hey, me too. I helped them to see that despite whatever differences we might have, I had the same goals in terms of meeting my earnings targets, managing my staff, and so forth. One by one, I showed them that even though I was the first African-American in their "club" of company presidents, they could judge me as they judged the rest of their peers—by my performance. That took the awkward feeling out of our conversations. They began to relax around me and we started building relationships of trust. I wasn't a white executive, but they accepted me as an executive who was different but still belonged in the club.

As I developed these relationships with the other top players in the industry, I had the chance to share with them that my company was selling far more black gospel music than anyone had believed possible. They noticed that we were having success marketing to the African-American community in ways their companies hadn't tried. They wanted to learn more about our approach. That was the promise of mutual benefit I showed them, and as I did so, a long list of benefits began to result for our community.

For the first time, the people who controlled the purse strings in other companies were willing to put more resources into marketing black gospel music. There was more attendance by other companies at black gospel events and more participation by gospel people on Christian music industry boards. More record company resources were spent on conferences and events geared to primarily African-American audiences. Labels that had never had a presence in the gospel industry began putting out gospel music and hiring African-American executives at the highest levels. That nonsense about changing the name of the Gospel Music Association was put aside, and the entire black gospel industry, from the pastors to the small recording companies to the tastemakers in the African-American media, were all treated with greater respect. These changes led to more new and successful business ventures, and in time even people who didn't pay attention to music at all came to admire gospel as a viable business.

Some opened their minds for all of what I personally considered the right reasons, some just for the financial opportunity; but as more and more people saw what was in it for them, the cycle of success kept intensifying, not just for me or my company but for the entire industry. We all shared a genuine desire to grow the business and that was enough. Black gospel music grew exponentially and the community thrived.

Only then, after I had gained the trust and involvement of others in the industry, and after the benefits of our business relationships were clear to everyone, did I work to address segregation in the business directly. I founded a task force on race for the music industry, to continue the conversation, but even then the primary emphasis was on business. I wanted to give people in the industry a chance to talk about what the patterns of behavior had been in the past—choices made by white executives, attitudes of black executives—and the consequences of that behavior and those attitudes for the growth of the music business. Now we had a safe place to hold a more challenging discussion.

CHANGING MINDS GROWS THE BUSINESS

SO FAR IN THIS chapter I've described ways in which changing people's assumptions can make it possible to solve a range of problems within and across organizations. But one type of problem is so crucial to every business that it deserves special attention: how to keep a business growing. Every successful business reaches the point where growth slows because the company or the industry has already tapped most of the customers in its original customer base. To keep growing, it must either find new products that existing customers want or reach beyond its established customers to find new ones. What was Martha Stewart doing at Kmart? She had realized that there wasn't much more room to find new customers for her home goods in the luxury market, so she brought her style to a more general audience. In the same way, beginning in the 1990s, it gradually became clear across all of professional sports that growth among white male fans was slowing; to keep growing the audience, it would be necessary to appeal to a wider range of potential fans, including women, African-Americans, and Latinos.

To do these sorts of things, you have to change minds. You have to take people who have not been fans of Martha Stewart or major league baseball or whatever organization you want to grow, and help them to see that organization differently. You have to convince people within the organization to work to make the newcomers feel welcome. But right away, you run into some old assumptions: "These new customers have never supported us before." "It can't be done." Even people within your organization who might benefit from a new sales approach or an expanded audience or customer base get stuck in a kind of chicken-and-egg paradox: which comes first?

I ran into these kinds of assumptions when I started to make the case that NASCAR, like any other professional sport, could only continue to grow by widening its appeal to a more varied audience. We already had a bigger variety of fans than most people realized—over 40 percent of our audience, for example, was female—but I knew we could go further. Still, I kept hearing from the doubters. Their argument went something like this: "Sure, it might be nice to have more women fans and more fans of color watching the races, but the fans won't show up until we have drivers who look like them. New drivers can't show up until we have more sponsors to pay for their cars and crews, and sponsors won't show until we have more fans to buy their products and services. Which comes first? Frankly, Max, you've got no chicken and you've got no eggs; you can't grow NASCAR's business by diversifying. It's impossible."

This talk about why we "couldn't" succeed took me back to my early days, when Mickey Carter and I were trying to get started as talent agents. As newcomers to our chosen work, we faced the same sort of chicken-and-egg paradox: what would come first? We had no track record, so why should clients trust us? We had no clients, so how could we prove we were qualified to do this kind of work? Maybe the whole thing was impossible. So what did we do? We used what we had to try to jump-start the cycle of success: I called my sister, who got us one meeting, which led to one client who began to tell people about our track record. That got us more clients, which got us more credibility; and in time the cycle of success started rolling. One day we found we had lots of chickens and lots of eggs—and people stopped asking us which came first.

Back in chapter 4, when I described the cycle of success, I was talking about a process by which you could build on individual achievements to grow your career. Now I want to make the point that a similar cycle of success can develop on a much larger scale, between any business and its customers. Just as in an individual career, small successes can build credibility; credibility inspires more people to take a chance; more chances, met with excellence, lead to greater successes; and the cycle feeds on itself. But now, on this larger scale, you're not working only for yourself, you're serving—whether in a small or large way—as one of the ambassadors who help your project or business to grow its customer base.

In that role, there are three principles to bear in mind. Let's take them one at a time.

1. **People don't need to agree all the way to succeed with you all the way.** I've talked a lot in this book about finding common interests and common ground, but it's just as important to realize that while you need common ground to stand on—some area of agreement and mutual benefit—it doesn't have to be big. People who disagree on a lot of things can still succeed together. For that reason, I want to give an example of a success we had in diversifying NASCAR to grow the business. The point of the story is not that everyone came to see things the same way. The point is that there was plenty of disagreement and plenty of difference in goals, but there was just enough agreement to move things forward.

   In 2009, a young African-American driver named Michael Cherry was competing at the South Boston Speedway in Virginia. He was a talented driver but so far he lacked the sponsorship to move to the next level of racing. On that day, though, he caught the eye of team owner Blair Addis. Addis admired Cherry's control of his car and saw something unique in his driving style. He was impressed by the way that Cherry, who had worked on cars with his father since he was eight years old, knew the workings of the car itself; he was also impressed by his comfort in front of a camera. (Before getting into racing, Cherry had been a successful child actor.) Based on the talent and skill he observed at the Drive for Diversity event, Addis asked Cherry to move from his home in Florida up to Greenville, South Carolina, so Cherry could be part of the day-to-day operation of the Addis Motorsports race shop while competing every week in the late-model car series.

   But in this case, there was more than the usual connection between a promising driver and a lower-tier team. When

Addis went to his local insurance office to make a deposit on an electric bill for Cherry, he got into a conversation with the insurance agent, Carlo White, about the team's new driver. What happened next shows how the cycle of success begins to move. Carlo White, an African-American, was not a NASCAR fan, but he was interested in growing Nationwide Insurance's business. He sat on the company's diversity committee. So the team owner pitched the insurance agent the idea of sponsoring Cherry's car, and White brought the idea to Nationwide, leading to a sponsorship deal for Cherry that included Nationwide's corporate and local offices.

The benefits were mutual. For Nationwide Insurance, becoming a sponsor of an African-American driver brought them new appeal with potential African-American clients, a group they were actively pursuing; for White, having his company name on a stock car gave him a personal advantage in making sales to the traditional NASCAR fan base, because he could connect with fans around their passion for the sport. Cherry of course got sponsorship and publicity, helping to establish him as an up-and-coming star. Finally, White became one of our biggest ambassadors to the African-American community, talking about the benefits the sport offers for businesspeople of color. Everyone involved found that the focus on diversity helped bring their business to the next level. But what's so important about this story, to me, is how little they had in common to begin with. Carlo White wasn't a NASCAR fan; Blair Addis was just looking out for his own company's interests; Michael Cherry had no relationship with either of them. But they found enough common ground for all three to grow their businesses.

2. What unites people to grow a business is a culture of excellence. On the personal level, there are many ways to bring people together. So many different interests and sympathies can help you put people at ease and bring them together

to socialize. But when you are trying to grow a business, no matter what the size, there is one essential piece of common ground: everyone wants the business to succeed. That's why, whatever your long-term goals, you need to start by bringing a business together around a shared culture of excellence.

When I took over NASCAR's Drive for Diversity program, known as D4D, I inherited a program with goals I admired personally: to increase the number of people of color and women in the pipeline to become drivers and crew members in NASCAR racing at all levels. But when I took over, D4D was failing to unite the industry around those goals. Some in the industry didn't see the point of a diversity initiative. Some who agreed with the overall goal were critical of the specific execution because drivers who came through the two-year program had not progressed to the top levels of stock car racing—it was as if they could play in the minor leagues but never get to the majors. To some, the failure of D4D "graduates" to land top jobs in NASCAR proved that the program should be scrapped, or replaced with a much smaller program that picked one or two minority or women drivers and paid their expenses—essentially creating a little quota in the sport. What struck me, however, was that everyone was making the same assumption, that the moral vision that had inspired D4D was all it had to draw on. I thought, instead, that it was time to emphasize excellence and the mutual goals of everyone involved.

Until then, the program had lacked contact with the top-tier NASCAR teams. So we reached out to them to learn what standards and tools they actually used to select their rookie drivers and new pit-crew members. Our plan was to give each year's D4D class clear, real-life goals to strive for, along with some time and money to realize their potential to reach those goals. It was like a college scholarship: two years to study with the best and then you were on your own. We brought in established women drivers and drivers of color to provide enrichment and tutoring. We offered the young drivers media training, so they could learn to present themselves most favorably during interviews to attract and retain sponsors. The way I saw it, we didn't need to pick out one or two of the best, because we already had the greatest mechanism in the world for recognizing excellence in drivers and crew: the race track itself. We would give them a chance to excel there and the rest would be up to them.

Now we had the involvement of the top-tier teams and we had the excitement of a program with the potential to discover genuine stars. Instead of downsizing D4D to a little quota program, we upgraded to a large program that offered true opportunity for talent and dedication to shine through. And we started to see results: Michael Cherry—who landed the Nationwide Insurance sponsorship—was one of our D4D drivers, and his success brought newfound media attention to the successes of drivers of color, helping to grow the sport's audience and its reach with sponsors. The cycle of success had turned again.

3. **Crises and setbacks may be your best chance for real dialogue.** Whenever you set out to change minds, you can expect some difficulty along the way. A disappointing result or a provocative incident can threaten to shut conversation down entirely. But in fact, those moments are often your best chance to speak honestly about the problems that have emerged, to show people all you have in common and to make clear what you can gain by working together.

For example, when the downturn in the economy began in 2008, it hit Dale Earnhardt Inc. at a time of transition, and like many teams we had to downsize to survive. During my years as president I supervised two different mergers, and as jobs became redundant in the combined companies, I personally was responsible for laying off over a hundred talented and devoted employees. It was one of the most wrenching experiences I've ever had, and hardest of course on those who lost their jobs. To me, that was another example of how in life, and at any level of business, things don't necessarily go according to our plan. But one result was that the other team owners and presidents, many of whom faced similarly challenging situations, saw that I was going through the same difficulties that they faced. We were drawn together to commiserate and to share experiences. The relationships and goodwill that I developed as we went through that trial by fire helped me when I took over the Drive for Diversity program. As I've said, I wanted even the top-tier teams to participate, but I had no authority over them—in NASCAR, every team and even every track is independent. What I did have was the relationships that were strengthened by the difficulties we went through together, and I drew on those relationships as I worked to grow the D4D program from a promising idea into a practical success.

CHANGING MINDS LETS YOU LIVE YOUR VISION

SO FAR, I'VE TALKED about the reasons your business or group will benefit when you work to change minds and uplift the community. But there is someone else who needs you to learn to change minds and uplift the community—you. Why? This approach allows you to unite your personal vision with the practical demands of your life. In other words, changing people's minds while uplifting the community is a way to find and to live your purpose, with all the benefits, practical and spiritual, a purposeful life brings.

In the preface of this book I described my first clear moment of vision, how I saw myself dressed in good enough clothes and shoes that people would stop prejudging me based on how I was dressed. That vision guided me to success in some of my early jobs, working as a short-order cook and as a bank teller. Success there allowed me in turn to aspire to new levels of accomplishment, such as a college degree, continuing the cycle of success. But in addition to that practical success, I was also discovering another kind of cycle, one you might call the cycle of spiritual success. I found that my vision could lead me where I needed to go and that I could rely on certain spiritual teachings in my everyday life.

In time, my spiritual vision also became more ambitious. Today, my vision is no longer to see myself in better clothes and shoes. It's to bring people from all walks of life together to succeed. That's the goal that drives my work, whether in sports or music, business or law. Of course, you have your own story and your own developing vision. But whatever it may be, you will find that when your work is true not just to your practical obligations but also to your passion, that is the most satisfying, reenergizing work there is.

How do you bring your private passions to work? You have to convince the people you work with that those passions have a place because they will do some good—in other words, you have to change their minds and show how your passions will uplift the community. Will that be easy? Maybe not at first. In the church, we often say that if God has given you a vision, chances are most other people won't get it, at least not right away. And if you're not careful, their lack of understanding can dull your own sense of your passion.

What can you do? To begin, I find it helps to set up your own purposeful routines, to strengthen your commitment to bringing your passions into the world and living according to your purpose, even when your day-to-day life may seem not to have any room for it.

1. Make acting according to your purpose and uplifting the community part of what you do regularly. Rather than waiting for the perfect job to express your purpose, look for small ways to make your commitment to that purpose an active, enjoyable part of your ordinary life. I believe my father

did this when he brought me along as he worked in the music industry. I absorbed his style of talking to people, his skills at putting them at ease, and his ways of blending business and personal relationships. I was just a little kid then, and it was unusual for a father to take a child to work for more than a quick visit, but he understood that there was a lot I could pick up even if I couldn't follow all the adult details. Sometimes I would just play cards with his colleagues; my Aunt Linda says that everyone who worked with her brother Bill knew that the rule was, "Max has to win." Looking back at those days, I think that might have helped to plant a powerful idea in the mind of that little boy from a broken home: he learned that he could walk into his father's business and win. In that way, my father brought his passion for his family to work.

With my own kids, I've tried to do the same thing, but in a way that is more sustained and, I hope, more fun for them. Out of all the different things I do, they have found a special inter- est in the musical performers I encounter, so I've helped them to start their own "company" around that interest. They call it Siegel Kids Entertainment, and the mission they've chosen for the company is to create informative videos for other kids. The idea is that by interviewing celebrities from a child's perspec- tive and seeing them through kids' eyes, they can create videos that speak to what children care about, rather than some adult's idea of what children would like to see. My kids come up with the overall concept for each segment and the interview ques- tions; they shoot the interviews and put it all together with a little input and guidance from their parents when they feel they need it.

To get them started, I helped them decide on the goals of the company, who the officers would be, how often they would hold company meetings, and who would be present at the meetings. I got them business cards. I send e-mails to make sure I get the minutes of each meeting, and to remind them that if they need help getting minutes written down, they can ask for it. When the weekend comes around, they are the ones who ask me, "Are we having a meeting this week, Dad?"

We started the company when the children were nine, seven, and five, and the beautiful thing was to see them learning about entrepreneurship, accountability, and what it takes to make a business work in a way we could all enjoy. "Working" with them refreshes my sense of how good it is to bring people together and help them to succeed at something they enjoy. Of course, in guiding them in this direction I drew from my own experience, and your experiences may be very different. But anyone who spends time with children or who volunteers time with adults could do something similar based on his or her own passions and skills, whatever they may be. And when you have the habit of uplifting the community in place, even in a small way, it helps to ready you for when the opportunity comes to follow the cycle of success to the next level.

2. Put your vision into words. For individuals as for organizations, it's easy to get caught up in the day-to-day details and to lose touch with what moves you. Even when I sit down with companies working on statements of values, I see how easily they get distracted by operational planning and strategic goals. They lose track of the larger purpose of what they do. That's why I believe that any company, group, or individual should make time, now and then, to articulate their vision as they understand it in the present.

We need to keep asking ourselves:

- Why am I doing all this?
- What are the practical reasons?
- What are the *impractical* reasons—what is the higher purpose

behind what I do? Why am I so passionate about it? (If I work with new media technology, I might do it because the technology is cool and fun. It also pays my rent. But beneath that, I may feel a passion for getting ordinary people the chance to join in the bigger conversation by setting them up with inexpensive but powerful technologies.)

- How do my everyday efforts connect to what matters most to me?
- What might take me away from achieving my vision?
- How can my vision help uplift my community, and how could I show others that this is true?
- What could I do more of to be in harmony with my purpose?

These questions are not self-indulgence. They are not a side interest or a little "extra" charitable something to do when time allows. They are at the heart of a successful life—your means to refresh your feeling for what makes you tick and to see more clearly what makes others tick. By answering these questions, you can find the energy and commitment to give your best and draw others together to work with you to reach your goals—both your practical goals and the goals that serve your higher purpose. Others who join with you may not realize for a while that you are serving a higher purpose, but as you succeed together you will have the chance to share more of what moves you by showing how it is a part of your passion and your practical success.

When you change people's assumptions in this way, you will discover that we can each live in harmony with our own purpose while uplifting the community we share. That has been my goal throughout my life, and it was my higher purpose in writing this book. I hope it serves you in reaching your goals, as well.

ACKNOWLEDGMENTS

I want to thank God for His grace, mercy, and provision.

I want to thank my wife, Jennifer, and my children, Max II, Matthew, and Madeline, who are my most powerful source of inspiration, the purpose for my drive and the reason I live. Thank you for being who you are and unselfishly sharing me with the world.

I want to thank my siblings, James, Jerry, Traci, and Ryan. We share a bond only our circumstances could make us appreciate.

I want to thank everyone who has made a significant contribution to my personal progress. While you all are too many to name, I want you to know that without you, I could not be who I am. And I am going to spend the rest of my life letting you know who you are and how much I appreciate you.

I would also like to thank G. F. Lichtenberg, my cowriter; Dawn Davis, my editor; Laura Nolan, my agent; and Janet Hill, who first believed in this project.

Finally, I want to acknowledge those who contributed to this book in ways big and small. Thank you all for your help in bringing this vision to life.

About the Author

An influential executive in the entertainment and sports industries, Max Siegel made history as the highest-ranking African-American executive in NASCAR when he became President of Global Operations at Dale Earnhardt Inc. Before that, he held dual titles at Sony/BMG, serving as both president of Zomba Gospel and senior vice president of Zomba Label Group, where he helped the company score more gold and platinum records than ever before. He is now head of NASCAR's Drive for Diversity program and producer of *The Ride*, the NASCAR reality show on BET/MTV. The coauthor of *About My Father's Business: Merging Ministry and Industry*, he splits his time between Charlotte, North Carolina, and Indianapolis, Indiana.

G. F. Lichtenberg is the author of *Playing Catch with My Mother*, a memoir, and coauthor of books on business, new media, self-help, and social issues. He is a professor in the Creative Writing Department of Columbia University.